THIS BOOK BELONGS TO:

SOUL FUEL for YOUNG EXPLORERS

BEAR GRYLLS

Illustrations by Patrick Laurent

HODDER FAITH YOUNG EXPLORERS

First published in Great Britain in 2020 by Hodder & Stoughton
An Hachette UK company
14
Copyright © BGV Global Limited, 2019 Introduction ©2020

Material originally published in Soul Fuel in Great Britain in 2019 by Hodder & Stoughton
This edition compiled and edited for a younger audience in 2020. Illustrations and page
design by Patrick Laurent © Hodder and Stoughton, 2020

The right of BGV Global Limited to be identified as the Author of the Work has been
asserted by them in accordance with the Copyright, Designs and Patents Act 1988.

A CIP catalogue record for this title is available from the British Library

Hardback ISBN 978 1 529 34774 6
eBook ISBN 978 1 529 34776 0

Printed and bound in Great Britain by Clays Ltd, Elcograf. S.p.A.

Hodder & Stoughton policy is to use papers that are natural, renewable and recyclable
products and made from wood grown in sustainable forests. The logging and
manufacturing processes are expected to conform to the environmental regulations of
the country of origin.

Hodder & Stoughton Ltd
Carmelite House
50 Victoria Embankment
London EC4Y 0DZ
www.hodderfaith.com

The authorised representative in the EEA is Hachette Ireland, 8 Castlecourt
Centre, Dublin 15, D15 XTP3, Ireland (email: info@hbgi.ie)

REMEMBER THIS:

You have a light within you, the Holy Spirit, and wherever you go you will bring a light greater than the darkness around you.

The Life-light blazed out of the darkness;
The darkness couldn't put it out.

John 1:5 MSG

CONTENTS

1. Where it all Started   **7**
It's all about faith in Jesus

2. A Bigger Picture   **31**
Living with purpose and hope

3. The Power Within   **55**
Living with vision, courage and determination

4. Living Well with Others   **79**
Relationships and forgiveness

5. Walking Humbly   **103**
Being faithful and enjoying God's faithfulness

6. True Freedom   **127**
How choosing God's wisdom and way brings freedom

7. To Adventure!   **151**
With the right foundations - risk is the key to growth

INTRODUCTION

Adventure has been the one constant through my life and it has taught me so much. Not only in terms of physical survival but also helping to empower my faith, friendships and attitudes.

The future belongs to you, young people, and my goal is always to do my best to inspire positive values for your life. That's the mission. To know the source and power of courage, resilience, wisdom and true vision. It is why I hope that within the pages of this book, you'll find many little nuggets to strengthen you day to day.

It's important for you to be encouraged to follow your dreams. They are often God given. Get out there and live your life with purpose, courage and passion. My father always inspired my adventurous streak and love of life, encouraging me to go that little bit extra in order to achieve my goals.

He reminded me that we have to fail many times before we succeed; that the key to life is always getting back on our feet.

My hope is that through these readings, I can shine a light on the truth that with faith, ambition and that never-give-up attitude, you really can achieve so much in your life.

That's what *Soul Fuel for Young Explorers* is really about. It's the chance to share with you the kind of fuel I rely on every day to try to keep me strong and keep me moving forward. Like a firesteel or a length of good rope, my faith is another essential tool in my survival gear. But it is so much more. It's my backbone, the heart of it all – the greatest source of any strength I have.

This book has fuel for your journey in its pages. Don't under-estimate the power of the words of the Bible. So often they have been light to a dark path for me.

As it says: 'Your word is a lamp for my feet, a light on my path.' (Psalm 119:105) I truly hope this book blesses you every day.

If nothing else, I want you to hear one message loud and clear:

FAITH IS A JOURNEY,

and like all great journeys it is made up of small, determined steps taken every day, in the love and light of the Almighty.

And never forget: He made you amazing.

Bear.

3

I WAS SIXTEEN WHEN IT HAPPENED.

It was the end of an ordinary school day, and as the last of the lights in our house were turned off and the darkness finally settled, I quietly slipped out of the ground-floor window.

I knew where I was going. To my favourite tree and my secret hideaway. I had always loved climbing high up into the sky, into her arms, hidden from view below by all the limbs and leaves beneath me.

The news that my godfather, Stephen, had died suddenly and without warning of a heart attack had hit me so hard. Stephen had been my father's best friend in the world, and he was like a second father to me.

He came on all our family holidays. He'd helped me learn to do so much and always laughed and cheered me on. His death felt as if someone had ripped my heart out.

I climbed quickly. The feel of the bark, the angle of the branches, the way the tree started to move with my weight the higher I got — it all felt familiar. And when I was forty feet up and had reached the last limb that I knew could hold me, I stopped.

AND THEN THE TEARS CAME.

And the anger. I held my head in my hands. I sobbed and hit the tree.

As the anger subsided for a few moments and the tears dried for a little while, I prayed the only prayer that ever really matters to the human heart: 'Jesus, if You are real, if You are there, please be beside me this night.'

WHERE IT ALL STARTED

NEVER ALONE

The Bible uses many names for Jesus, but 'Immanuel' is one of my favourites. It means 'God with us', and it's a statement of truth that you can build your life on.

I AM WITH YOU

Through His Spirit,
Jesus is always with us.

Think about it for a moment:

THE SAME GOD WHO CREATED THE UNIVERSE IS WITH US RIGHT NOW.

That's life changing, and it's not something to be taken lightly.

It doesn't mean that we get a free pass to miss all of life's hard times. God doesn't ever promise a trouble-free life. Life is a series of battles. But He does offer something even better: He promises to be with us.

'Because he loves me,' says the LORD, 'I will rescue him; I will protect him, for he acknowledges my name. He will call on me, and I will answer him; I will be with him in trouble.'

Psalm 91:14–15

This is what makes all the difference in life. Even in the darkest times, God is with us. Even when everything else appears lost, you are never alone. Ever.

TAKE Time

We can go roughly three weeks without food, three days without water and three minutes without oxygen. How long can we live effectively without refuelling our faith?

Jesus never went long without praying. There was a time when the crowds were so desperate to get a piece of Him that there was no time to eat. People were running towards Him, predicting where He might be going next and waiting there. It was the busiest season in His life, but Jesus knew that He needed time alone in prayer, even more so when it was busy. Jesus always seemed to stick to this routine as a clear source of power for the day ahead.

COME WITH ME BY YOURSELVES TO A QUIET PLACE AND GET SOME REST.

Mark 6:31

Jesus' words to His disciples are also words to us today. That's why I try my best to start every day in a quiet place, getting my soul fuel in, even if for just a few minutes. And do you know what? Whether it feels like it or not, I know He's always ready and waiting for me, and He's never late.

So make that little time each day and protect it. Breathe in; know His presence around you. Let His words soak in; let His strength empower you. Be thankful and pray for the day ahead. Be still and know that He is with you.

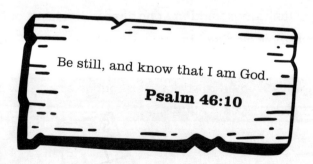

Be still, and know that I am God.

Psalm 46:10

Now we are ready to hit the day.

IT'S GOOD TO BE REMINDED

I have to walk through the door of fear regularly in my life. We all do if we are to get anywhere meaningful. But I have learned to pray quietly in my heart in those moments and to draw on Someone bigger, braver and stronger than I am. That's been the key. Don't go alone. Put your hand in the hand of the Almighty. He's there for us.

A lot of us try to keep our fears secret, but burying them is how they grow. When we bring them into the light, they often start to wither. But to bring them out and share them with God or loved ones takes courage.

That's what great fathers do. They hold their children's hands.

The prayers I say when I'm afraid are raw. (They are maybe not prayers in the sense I was taught at school. But they are real prayers.) I'm showing God my deepest fears and asking Him to be beside me. I'm asking Him for His help to keep me moving forward.

See what the Bible says:

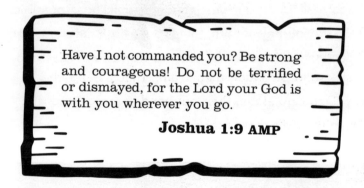

Have I not commanded you? Be strong and courageous! Do not be terrified or dismayed, for the Lord your God is with you wherever you go.

Joshua 1:9 AMP

Whatever fear we're facing, remember this: we do not face it alone. The Creator of the universe is good; He is beside us, within us and for us.

WHAT DOES GOD REQUIRE?

Any big journey often brings out mixed emotions at the start. A lot of the time we just want to hurry on and make it to our destination as quickly as possible. On the journey of faith, things are a little different. The destination is so far off that we won't even reach it in this lifetime. And the journey we take to get there is full of challenges. And it's long – so long that it will last beyond our final breath.

But here's the truth: we don't travel alone. God is both our destination and our guide, and He has promised to be with us every step of the way.

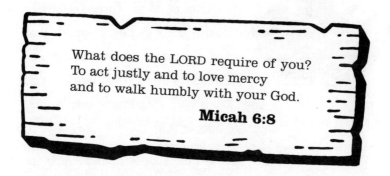

And what should those steps look like? The answer is beautifully clear:

> What does the LORD require of you?
> To act justly and to love mercy
> and to walk humbly with your God.
>
> **Micah 6:8**

You and I are definitely going to stumble from time to time, but when we do, let's not lose heart. Let's look up and see His hand outstretched above us, helping us back to our feet.

ACT JUSTLY, LOVE MERCY AND WALK HUMBLY WITH OUR GOD.

GOD MADE US ALL

Koko was forty-six when she died in her sleep. It was not a dramatic death, but it was reported around the world. You see, Koko was a gorilla – and a very unusual one at that.

When Penny Patterson, a PhD student, told her tutor that she wanted to see whether gorillas could learn sign language, she was told that it was unlikely. She decided to try anyway.

Even though Koko started slowly, learning just three words in four years, she finally got going. Eventually she learned more than one thousand words of sign language and could understand almost two thousand spoken words. She combined words when she needed to – calling a ring a 'finger bracelet' and nectarine yogurt 'orange flower sauce'.

 But the best signing she ever did was when a journalist asked her for the meaning of life.

'People be polite,' she signed. 'People have goodness."

I love Koko's explanation of the meaning of life – and it seems a lot like the greatest commandment Jesus gave us: to love the Lord your God with all your heart and to love your neighbour as yourself (Matthew 22:36–9). Be polite. Have goodness.

It's funny how so much of science and the natural world is intertwined with humanity, instinctively working in harmony.

Look at what the Bible says:

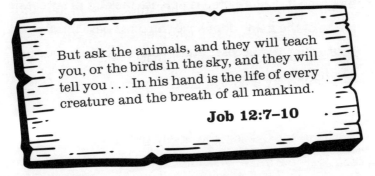

But ask the animals, and they will teach you, or the birds in the sky, and they will tell you . . . In his hand is the life of every creature and the breath of all mankind.

Job 12:7–10

God made us all. The animals, the stars, the whole world. But we humans, His children, will always have the most special place in His heart.

FORTRESS from FAILURE

At some point in your life, you're going to fail big-time, especially if you set for yourself significant goals or follow your calling towards some big old mountains.

Failure will be part of your journey. Don't fear it; embrace it. Failure means you are making progress. It is one of the many doorways you must pass through on your route to success. But failure, rejection, mockery and humiliation hurt.

At times like these, it's good to remember the words of people like King David, a man who failed spectacularly and regularly. He was indeed a man who knew all about God's love and grace.

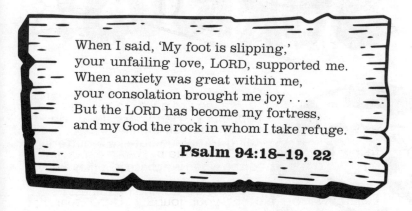

When I said, 'My foot is slipping,'
your unfailing love, LORD, supported me.
When anxiety was great within me,
your consolation brought me joy . . .
But the LORD has become my fortress,
and my God the rock in whom I take refuge.

Psalm 94:18–19, 22

We can always turn to God for help and comfort in our failures. The power of failure evaporates in His presence.

WhY so SeRIOUS?

The whole world is seeking happiness. Happiness is a good thing to pursue but like a butterfly, often when we chase it, it flies away. So how do we find happiness?

The Bible shows us how both laughter and joy lead to an enriched life. Where laughter and joy are, so also there will be happiness. And the Bible reminds us that 'a cheerful heart is good medicine' (Proverbs 17:22).

Let's not take ourselves too seriously. We need to laugh at situations – and ourselves. Laughter is like an internal workout.

It exercises our spirit and helps keep our hearts and minds healthy. (By the way, my mum and dad used to say 'Laugh with people; not at people.' That was good advice.)

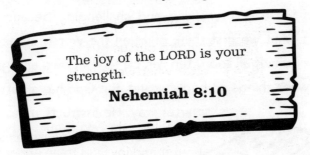

And what about joy? What is it? Joy runs deep and is less transient than just happiness. Joy goes beyond simply a pleasing emotion – joy brings peace, strength and light. Joy goes right down to the heart of our very being.

> The joy of the LORD is your strength.
> **Nehemiah 8:10**

Laughter, happiness and joy. These might sound like simple things, but don't underestimate their power to bring life and light to all around you. No doubt Jesus laughed a lot, and happiness and joy were at the heart of how He lived.

Jesus knew great sorrow and great pain, but I often think that if we were to meet Him in the flesh, part of what we would remember most would be His sense of fun and laughter. I like that.

Be Thankful

**Give thanks in all circumstances;
for this is God's will for you.
1 Thessalonians 5:18**

This verse is interesting and challenging because it isn't what we first think of when the worst happens! Our default all too often can be to fall down and give up when things go badly wrong. But God has a better, smarter way. He instructs us to be grateful in all circumstances. Instead of blaming and wailing, give thanks for all the good in your life. That's radical living.

The deepest 'good' is the truth that we are loved by God and given a future with Him for eternity. That in itself is crazy good news.

It is scientifically proven that gratitude changes our health and mind for the better. So let's make this a daily attitude and way to live: always in

gratitude for our blessings, whether it be food, health, relationships, fun, family or simply His promises for our future.

Paul knew all about this too:

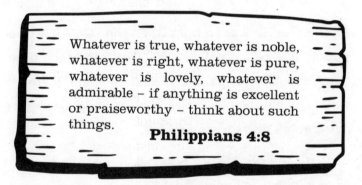

Whatever is true, whatever is noble, whatever is right, whatever is pure, whatever is lovely, whatever is admirable – if anything is excellent or praiseworthy – think about such things.

Philippians 4:8

In other words, look for the positive and choose to be grateful. He was right. When we look around us and focus on all that is good, it helps us see God in so many of the little things that we often overlook, whether it be the leap of a dog in delight at seeing us, or the smile and kindness of a teacher. Christ is in it all. When we live like this, it is as though our eyes are being opened. And it starts with gratitude.

JESUS LOVES US WHEN WE are Broken

Mother Teresa was so right when she said, 'The poor people are very great people. They can teach us so many beautiful things. We must know them, there are very loveable people, they are great people, they are Jesus in the distressing disguise.'[2]

Love for the poor is not optional. It is at the heart of what it means to know Christ.

When we spot someone showing love to others who are on the outside – like Mother Teresa did – it's evidence of living faith.

Her words echo Jesus in Matthew 25 when He said:

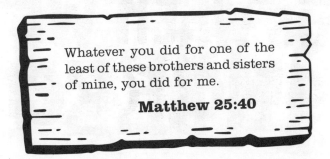

Whatever you did for one of the least of these brothers and sisters of mine, you did for me.

Matthew 25:40

When you read the stories about Jesus, it's good to notice where He is and who He's with. There are a few temples and religious leaders in there, but much of the time He's with the outcasts, the poor, the overlooked and the downtrodden. He's with the people everybody knows are messing up.

If you want to see Him at work today, go and join with others who are showing His love to ones the rest of the world so often overlook.

POOR OUT CASTS OVER LOOKED DOWN TROD DEN

FRIEND INDEED

Does God need us to be strong? No. Does He need us to be impressive? Definitely not. God is not wowed by our abilities. He goes where He is welcome and needed. He's looking for people who say a quiet yes to Him in their hearts. Those who understand that alone we are so limited. When we are empty, He can fill us and work through us.

WHEN WE THINK WE HAVE IT ALL IN HAND OURSELVES THERE IS NO ROOM IN OUR HEARTS FOR HIM TO WORK HIS MIRACLES.

Jesus said:

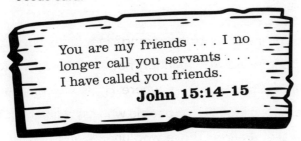

You are my friends . . . I no longer call you servants . . . I have called you friends.

John 15:14–15

There is nothing more empowering – and no greater privilege in life – than to be called a friend of the Almighty.

IN THE SUMMER OF 1996,

I went skydiving with friends during a military trip to South Africa.

The flight to fifteen thousand feet was uneventful. Soon I stood in the cargo area of the plane and looked down. I took a familiar deep breath, then slid off the step. At four thousand feet I pulled the ripcord and heard the canopy open with a reassuring crack. My 130-mph free fall quickly slowed down to 25 mph, just as it always did.

But when I looked up I realised something was wrong – very wrong. Instead of a smooth rectangular shape above me, I had a very deformed-looking tangle of chute, which meant the whole parachute would be a nightmare to try to control. I pulled hard on both steering toggles to see if that would help me.

It didn't.

I dropped away and smashed into the desert floor, landing on my back.

I couldn't stand up; I could only roll over and moan on the dusty earth. I was biting the ground in agony.

Sometimes it isn't until we get knocked down that we find which way is up. Sometimes it isn't until the sky clouds over that we notice the light. And sometimes it isn't until we lie in the gutter that we begin to see the stars.

The light of God has been the greatest source of hope this world has ever known. We can never be so far away that the light won't reach us. Sometimes it is good to be reminded of that.

I had smashed my back in three places, but miraculously I hadn't been paralysed. I had survived for a reason.

Over time as I recovered in a military rehabilitation centre, I felt life calling me to grab it and to live it: to throw myself in feet first, 120 per cent; to get out there and take risks; to fail and get back up; to laugh at the setbacks and at myself; to explore; to try never to give up. After all, I had come so close to losing it all, right?

GOD WORKS THROUGH THE STORMS OF OUR LIVES, AND TOUGH TIMES SO OFTEN MEAN FRESH BEGINNINGS WITH A NEW PURPOSE AND HOPE.

A BIGGER PICTURE

TACKLING LIFE

How can we tackle huge projects without getting overwhelmed? How can we face even the smallest of tasks when often we just don't feel able? In the Bible book of Judges, Gideon was chosen by God to be a military leader. His response was very human: he was riddled with fear.

'"But Lord," Gideon asked, "how can I save Israel? My clan is the weakest in Manasseh, and I am the least in my family." The LORD answered, "I will be with you . . ."' (Judges 6:15–16).

The same promise that God made to Gideon is repeated by Jesus to us (I had this verse engraved on the inside of Shara's wedding ring when we were first married. It's a good 'un!):

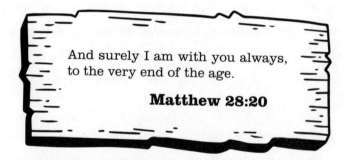

And surely I am with you always, to the very end of the age.

Matthew 28:20

IF WE WANT EMPOWERED LIVES,

we have to start with the knowledge and trust that God is with us, ready to guide and strengthen our steps each day. Be confident in that simple life-changing truth, because it changes everything.

Don't Go it Alone

We all have days when we feel as though we don't match up to other people. We all experience times when we're unsure what move to make next, and none of us will go through life without experiencing fear at some time.

Gideon faced all of this. Thankfully, it didn't matter that he was lacking in self-confidence. He had God-confidence instead. In fact, just to make sure he didn't try to find confidence anywhere else, God reduced Gideon's army from twenty-two thousand men to just three hundred!

It's a vital lesson to take on. If we put our hearts and trust and confidence in God, He will work through us powerfully – just as He did through Gideon. God does not need large numbers.

He just needs willing hearts.

When we give that, we gain the greatest power:

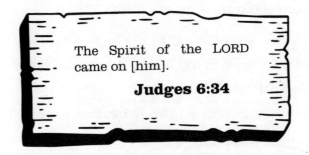

The Spirit of the LORD came on [him].

Judges 6:34

Whatever today holds for us, we all need the light and love of God to help us in our relationships and encounters. We need Him to give us the power to fulfil the calling He has for us. We can't go it alone, and we're not designed to. Stay in the power zone: less of our frail attempts; more of His strength in everything we do.

BROKEN POTS

A water bearer in India had two large pots, one hung each end of a pole that was slung across his neck. One of the pots was perfect and always delivered a full portion of water.

The other was cracked. At the end of the long walk from the stream to the house, the cracked pot always arrived half full.

The broken pot was embarrassed and miserable. One day, while the water bearer was filling it up at the stream, the pot spoke: 'I am ashamed of myself, and I want to apologise to you.

I have only been able to deliver half of what you give me because of this crack in my side. I leak all the way back to your house, making extra work for you.'

The water bearer smiled. 'Haven't you noticed the flowers that are growing on only your side of the path? I've always known about your crack, and so I planted flower seeds on your side of the path, not the other. You've watered them every day without realising it.'[3]

You don't need to be perfect for God to use you. You just need to be available.

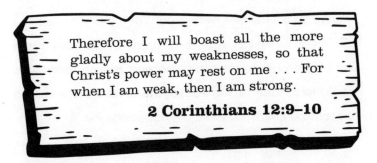

Therefore I will boast all the more gladly about my weaknesses, so that Christ's power may rest on me . . . For when I am weak, then I am strong.

2 Corinthians 12:9–10

As we focus less on ourselves, and more on our need for God's help and presence, we create space to receive the light of God. Our flaws and hurts allow Christ to shine through us, and they become a way for His love to reach others.

IN THE MIDST OF THE STORMS

The storm on the Sea of Galilee didn't just whip up the wind and the waves; it sent everyone in the boat into a panic. Even the hardened fishermen among them who would have been used to bad weather were reduced to terrified children. Well, almost everyone.

As the disciples panicked and prayed, Jesus stayed asleep. The disciples were only too aware of the danger and the risk. They knew that waves of that size could overturn their boat and take their lives.

Jesus stayed asleep.

Two thousand years later, we are still so often found panicking in the boat. When life gets tough we can spend a lot of time and energy wondering when Jesus is going to wake up and do something! In times like these, our faith is being tested.

Eventually Jesus acted, and the storm was silenced as quickly as it came. He calmed the wild sea that was raging around and within the disciples.

Quiet! Be still!
Mark 4:39

He's still the same Lord, and He's still got the same power to calm the winds, the waves and the panic within us. He still has the power to take a story that begins with fear and end it with faith.

Learn to look to Jesus, to trust Him even in the middle of the fiercest of life's storms. And like a muscle, as we work it, it gets ever stronger. This is how men and women of faith are made: they live in the knowledge that God protects them.

Created for Good Works

When a journey doesn't unfold the way we planned, we often start wondering, Have I strayed too far from my original course? Am I heading in the wrong direction?

Sometimes it's good to stop and check, especially on the journey of faith. From time to time we all need to be reminded of the fact that we are human – we stray off course and we fall down. But life is about being willing to humble ourselves; it's about acknowledging our failing and then standing back up, leaning on God's strength and His supply. And then, as the Scouts say, do your best.

When we do this, good things follow.

GOD NEVER FORCES HIMSELF
INTO OUR LIVES.

He works where there are willing, available hearts. He isn't looking for strong hearts, but willing hearts – hearts and lives that are open to Him coming alongside and leading us into life and light.

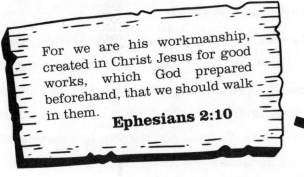

For we are his workmanship, created in Christ Jesus for good works, which God prepared beforehand, that we should walk in them. **Ephesians 2:10**

Once we put our hand into His, then He can lead. And where He leads is always good – it's not always easy, but it is always good. That's faith and trust, and both are the source of all great power.

PROTECTED & PROTECTING

In the Psalms, David marvelled at the fact that human beings are the pinnacle of God's creation – a masterpiece – made in His image. God not only loves you and cares about you but has given you extraordinary privileges.

We have been put in charge of everything God has made. That's an incredible privilege. But it's also a powerful responsibility. Knowing this, we should be at the forefront of the protection, preservation and care of God's amazing creation. And that means the earth, the animals and all people.

How do we do that? We start by always knowing where our power comes from: closeness to Christ and dependence on His strength, His goodness and His peace. When we walk away from this, let's remember His love and care that is acting like a magnet, edging us back again to the shadow of His wings.

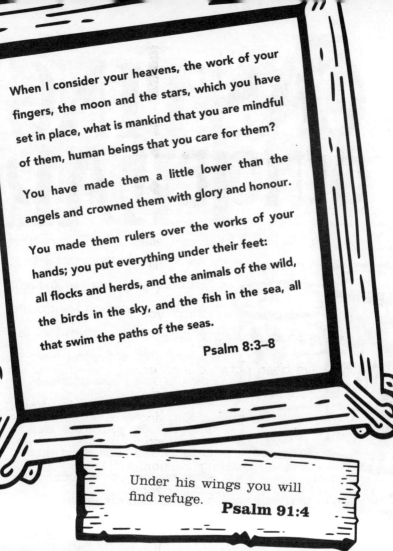

When I consider your heavens, the work of your fingers, the moon and the stars, which you have set in place, what is mankind that you are mindful of them, human beings that you care for them?

You have made them a little lower than the angels and crowned them with glory and honour.

You made them rulers over the works of your hands; you put everything under their feet: all flocks and herds, and the animals of the wild, the birds in the sky, and the fish in the sea, all that swim the paths of the seas.

Psalm 8:3–8

Under his wings you will find refuge. **Psalm 91:4**

BE BOLD: look at how you and your family's actions and choices affect the planet. Remember that everything you do, you do in partnership with the God who created it all so keep listening and talking to Him about it.

CASTING OUT FEAR

Fear is toxic to happiness. It can destroy our enjoyment of the present and suffocate any hope we have for the future. But it doesn't have to be this way. God promises to rescue you 'from hidden traps, [he] shields you from deadly hazards. His huge outstretched arms protect you – under them you're perfectly safe; his arms fend off all harm' (Psalm 91:3–4 MSG).

Have a read of Psalm 91 – look how fearless the author (the psalmist) is!

The psalmist told us to

'FEAR NOTHING'

(v. 5 MSG), and he went on to describe the kind of fearlessness we can all hope for: 'You will not fear the terror of night, nor the arrow that flies by day, nor the pestilence that stalks in the darkness, nor the plague that destroys at midday' (v. 5–6).

How do we get there? Perfect love casts out fear. When we are rooted in the love of God – the presence, strength and peace of God – we see beyond the fear. The closer we are to God, the weaker fear's grip becomes on us. As the psalmist wrote:

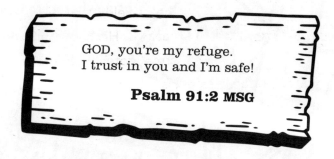

GOD, you're my refuge.
I trust in you and I'm safe!

Psalm 91:2 MSG

Fear doesn't have to have the last word or be the loudest voice within us. And it is God's love that always drives it away.

Stewards of Hope

Hope is so desperately needed in our world and it really matters where we find it.

We all see so many dead-end 'miracle' solutions around us that all too often lead us nowhere. I remember once hearing an old man say,

Choose wisely where you find your hope, as it will shape your life & future.

This verse is where I choose to find real hope today:

> The LORD will guide you always;
> he will satisfy your needs in a sun-scorched land and will strengthen your frame.
>
> **Isaiah 58:11**

TRUSTING IN CHRIST MAKES US HIS MESSENGERS,

His stewards of hope.

A pastor friend of mine once wrote: 'We steward the only message on planet earth that can give people what their hearts need most, which is hope. Hope that sins can be forgiven. Hope that prayers can be answered. Hope that the doors of opportunity, that seemed locked, can be opened. Hope that broken relationships can be reconciled. Hope that diseased bodies can be healed. Hope that damaged trust can be restored.'[4]

This hope of ours is powerful stuff, and we get to live it and radiate it out to others. That's pretty amazing.

GOD CONFIDENCE

People talk about wanting self-confidence. But this has its flaws. If all we trust in is ourselves, we will fail. History tells us this repeatedly – humans don't always get it right.

Instead of self-confidence, let's develop God-confidence. Be confident in Him and in these fundamental truths:

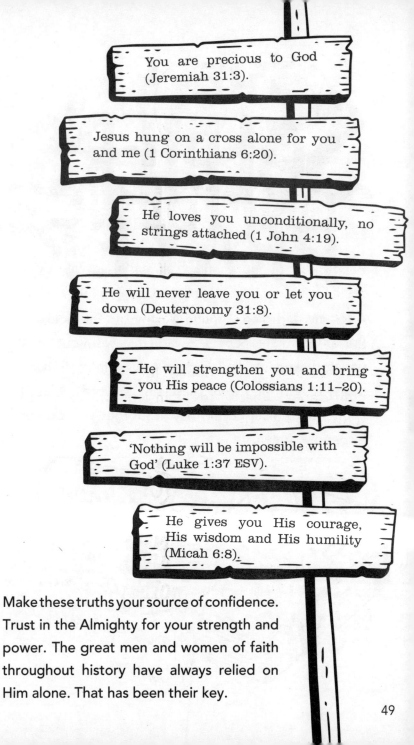

You are precious to God (Jeremiah 31:3).

Jesus hung on a cross alone for you and me (1 Corinthians 6:20).

He loves you unconditionally, no strings attached (1 John 4:19).

He will never leave you or let you down (Deuteronomy 31:8).

He will strengthen you and bring you His peace (Colossians 1:11–20).

'Nothing will be impossible with God' (Luke 1:37 ESV).

He gives you His courage, His wisdom and His humility (Micah 6:8).

Make these truths your source of confidence. Trust in the Almighty for your strength and power. The great men and women of faith throughout history have always relied on Him alone. That has been their key.

49

THE SOLDIER'S PRAYER

After my dad died, I found a copy of 'The Soldier's Prayer' among his papers. It was a thin, worn-out bit of paper, tucked into the side of his diary. In my father's messy handwriting were these simple words: 'Lord, I know what I must do this day. If I forget you, do not forget me. Amen.'

It was a humble reminder not only of his time serving as a commando but also of the faithful journey with Christ that my late father had travelled.

The longer we spend with God as our guide, the more our lives change. Day by day, we find ourselves overflowing with the things that really matter in life:

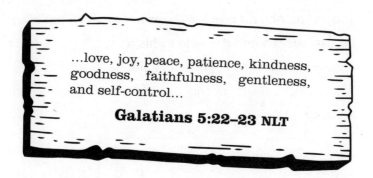

...love, joy, peace, patience, kindness, goodness, faithfulness, gentleness, and self-control...

Galatians 5:22–23 NLT

I saw this in my dad, and I see it in the lives of friends who quietly, humbly and faithfully bow their knee and follow Christ and His way of love. Let's aim to be full of the Holy Spirit, to overflowing, and faithful in our journey with Christ every day of our lives.

COURAGE ★ DETERMINATION ★ VISION

I will always remember the first SAS officer I ever met saying to me, 'Everyone who attempts Selection for the British Special Forces has the basic mark-one body: two arms, two legs, one head and one pumping set of lungs. What makes the difference between those who make it and those who don't is what goes on in here,' he said, touching his chest. 'Heart. . . that is what makes the big difference. Only you know if you have got what it takes.'

In the months that followed I had plenty of time to find out if I had what it took. Selection starts with a series of intense physical tests to weed out those who shouldn't have even applied: the long day and night marches across the mountains – carrying a heavy backpack, webbing and weapon – always against the clock, the weather, the terrain and your own doubts.

SAS

You were only safe if you gave 150 per cent, stayed near the front and never gave up.

It didn't get easier. If I wanted to make the grade, I had to push myself harder every week. But gradually something inside me changed; I was learning to get used to the pain. I was learning what living with determination and courage looked like.

Years later, I'm grateful for those lessons, and I'm still learning. The key to enduring for me was knowing that I had a strength I could rely on inside. The knowledge that however tired I felt, there was a Presence beside and within me that was edging me on, helping me stand, keeping me moving.

I always knew that this Presence was there, and it has never left me. Some call it God; some call it a universal force of power and love. Jesus lived in this force and shared it all day, every day. He said He was this force: 'I am the way and the truth and the life' (John 14:6), and I have learned through a lifetime of adventure that His promises for our lives and our future always hold true.

Take heart. Our journey of faith is just getting going, and we have the ultimate power and friend within us.

THE POWER WITHIN

Do Your BEST

Sometimes giving our all is hard. We can get tired, discouraged and fed up. At times like these, determination can be hard to come by. But if there's one thing that helps when you're battling through a difficult challenge, it's having someone beside you to cheer you on and offer encouragement. And that's exactly what God offers. Take a look at this passage:

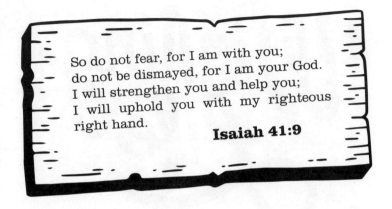

So do not fear, for I am with you;
do not be dismayed, for I am your God.
I will strengthen you and help you;
I will uphold you with my righteous
right hand.

Isaiah 41:9

When I was a soldier on Special Forces Selection, I used to repeat this line often to myself under my breath:

'I WILL STRENGTHEN YOU AND HELP YOU.'

As I struggled across the mountains carrying huge weights against the clock, those words had power, and His presence was always with me.

God tells us that He is 'our refuge and strength, an ever-present help in trouble' (Psalm 46:1). He's by our side, and that changes everything. On our own, doing our best is hard. But with God beside us, a whole world of possibilities opens up.

Winning Life

When learning to climb or to skydive, there's a process that we have to follow: we have to push through the difficult, awkward, unfamiliar part if we're going to develop the skills and results for the long haul.

Likewise, if we want to be fit and strong, we have to go through some tough training first.

The Bible is full of stories of great leaders whose tough beginnings served them well in the end. For Joseph and Daniel, being taken captive and shipped off to another land taught them about courage and built

a strong trust in God. That courage and trust stayed with them for their whole lives and allowed them to act wisely to the end.

COURAGE & TRUST

And then look at Jesus. He grew up within the brutality and corruption of Roman rule, but He grew up trusting God.

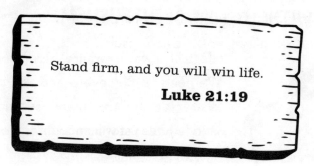

Stand firm, and you will win life.

Luke 21:19

It's hard sometimes to see beyond our present struggles, but we're not alone. Stand firm, trust, look up and have faith. Have courage and remember the pattern from those heroes before. With Christ within us, we can hold on and be faithful in the storms.

KEEP
GOING

→

Sir Winston Churchill is believed to have said,

'SUCCESS IS THE ABILITY TO MOVE FROM ONE FAILURE TO ANOTHER WITHOUT LOSS OF ENTHUSIASM.'

Life will always require hard work. We need to persevere and not get distracted by the many setbacks and failures we will encounter along the way.

No matter how strong or powerful we think we are, it is nothing compared to when we draw on the strength and power of Christ.

This is the task of the Holy Spirit: to keep us close to Christ, to help keep us going, to keep us kind, to keep us courageous – always driven on by love.

Whatever struggle we're facing

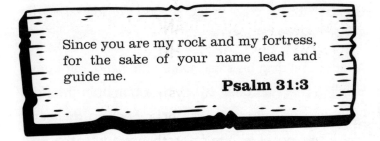

GOD IS THE ULTIMATE SOURCE of VICTORY.

and He is on our side.

> Since you are my rock and my fortress, for the sake of your name lead and guide me.
>
> **Psalm 31:3**

We gain incredible confidence when we lean on God. We don't have to pretend that we have it all together or that we are successful, strong and happy all the time.

Life is hard sometimes, but whatever we're facing, His hand of love is always there to help us, regardless of our feelings. Trust Him because He is good.

JUMP!

This story is told by a friend of mine, Pastor Nicky Gumbel. It took place in the Second World War, in the terrible days of the Blitz:

A father, holding his small son by the hand, ran from a building that had been struck by a bomb. In the front yard was an enormous shell hole. Seeking shelter as quickly as possible, the father jumped into the hole and held up his arms for his son to follow. Terrified, yet hearing his father's voice telling him to jump, the boy replied, 'I can't see you!' The father called to the silhouette of his son, 'But I can see you. Jump!' The boy jumped, because he trusted his father.[5]

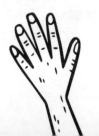

THE BOY LOVED HIM, HE BELIEVED IN HIM, HE TRUSTED HIM AND, HE HAD CONFIDENCE IN HIM.

...he rescues you from hidden traps, shields you from deadly hazards. His huge outstretched arms protect you – under them you're perfectly safe; his arms fend off all harm.

Psalm 91:3 MSG

Trust your heavenly Father's promises for your life. Trust that He has you, that He is in control, and that your future is secure in Him. Knowing these truths leads to courage, calm, confidence and power.

COURAGE
CALM
CONFIDENCE
POWER

IS IT WORTH IT?

Do you ever hear an Olympic gold medallist complain that the training wasn't worth it? Even if the race is over in a matter of seconds, the years of hard work and determined preparation are a small price to pay for the ultimate prize.

The apostle Paul understood this too. 'You've all been to the stadium and seen the athletes race. Everyone runs; one wins. Run to win. All good athletes train hard. They do it for a gold medal that tarnishes and fades. You're after one that's gold eternally' (1 Corinthians 9:24–5 MSG).

If sporting glories fade, how much more should we train and work hard for the prize of life? Paul wrote, 'I don't know about you, but I'm running hard for the finish line. I'm giving it everything I've got. No sloppy living for me! I'm staying alert and in top condition' (1 Corinthians 9:26 MSG).

But if there's one massive difference between athletes and us, as those who know Christ, it is this: this race is not won with just our own strength and abilities.

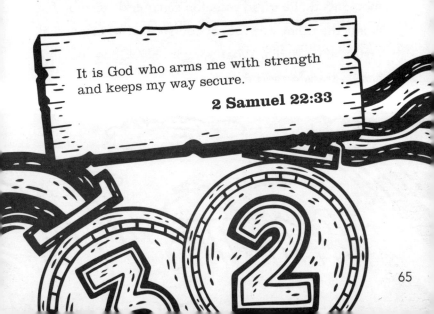

It is God who arms me with strength and keeps my way secure.

2 Samuel 22:33

Never Let Us Down. Never Let Us Drown.

Whenever I'm out in the wild, I always keep an eye on the sky. Conditions can shift so dramatically in a few moments that a good situation can quickly turn bad. It works the other way too, of course. Storms can end as fast as they begin. What appears bleak one moment can be transformed the next.

When we feel that situations are out of control and we are powerless to influence them, fear often follows. Look at the fear from the disciples when they were about to drown in a massive storm:

> 'Teacher, is it nothing to you that we're going down?'
> Mark 4:38 MSG

But it doesn't have to be that way, because Christ always gives us a safe place to turn to.

> Awake now, he told the wind to pipe down and said to the sea, 'Quiet! Settle down!' The wind ran out of breath; the sea became smooth as glass.
>
> **Mark 4:39–40 MSG**

Fear is natural, but where we turn to in those moments is what makes the difference. Life with Christ changes how we respond to tough situations. Turn with faith to the One who will never let us down and never let us drown.

ACTIVELY STILL

Fear is normal. In fact, a lot of the time it's needed. Fear keeps us sharp and is there to heighten our senses for battle. But uncontrolled, it can easily boil over into panic. And when that happens, our courage can evaporate like the morning mist.

Psalm 37 is full of great advice. 'Do not fret,' writes David – not just once or twice, but three times (vv. 1, 7, 8). He tells us to turn to the Lord, to bring Him our fears, and to trust in the Lord (v. 3).

So the response to fear and worry is to turn and to trust. Instead of letting fear overwhelm us, it can simply become a trigger to turn and to trust. To trust Christ is an active decision. It involves choosing to calm our thoughts, to slow our breathing and to look to Him. To trust takes courage, but it is the opposite of fear and panic.

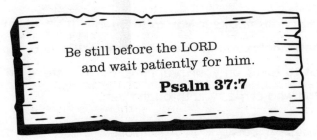

Be still before the LORD
and wait patiently for him.

Psalm 37:7

Being actively still – that's a cool concept. The presence of God brings calm and vanquishes fear. The good drowns out the bad, the light drives away the dark, and quiet confidence replaces panicked fear.

That's the way through fear.

SHELTER

Faith does not keep you from trouble. It's better than that: it helps you get through trouble. It's hard, but try not to focus on your problems. Focus instead on the One who carries you through them.

Wherever we are and whatever we're facing, we should always stay under His wing. We do that through an attitude of calm trust, passing any glory on to Him, because when we are sheltered under that wing, God gets the glory and God takes the flack.

That's why I love this psalm. It's God-focused, optimistic and so full of fuel for life:

I lift up my eyes to the mountains – where does my help come from?

My help comes from the LORD, the Maker of heaven and earth.

He will not let your foot slip – he who watches over you will not slumber;

indeed, he who watches over Israel will neither slumber nor sleep.

The LORD watches over you – the LORD is your shade at your right hand;

the sun will not harm you by day, nor the moon by night.

The LORD will keep you from all harm – he will watch over your life;

the LORD will watch over your coming and going both now and forevermore.

Psalm 121

Shelter with God. Be close to Him and trust Him to lead because He is good.

The Rope

As a young boy climbing with my dad, sometimes I would look up at a sheer rock face and feel that to climb it would be impossible. So often I would feel crippled and immobile with fear. But once that rope was connected between us, everything changed. Suddenly the impossible was possible and the fear turned to confidence.

As His children, being close to God has the same effect on us. We all get scared by different things. I'm a bit of an introvert at heart, so stormy seas or lonely mountains cause me less fear than a party full of people clinking glasses. But whatever our fears, the answer is the same: 'GOD takes care of all who stay close to him' (Psalm 31:23 MSG).

Even when things are difficult, keep looking up.

ASK OUR FATHER FOR HELP.

Listen to His calm voice over us: 'Be strong. Don't give up' (v. 24 MSG). Christ is on our side. He protects us (v. 20b) and hears us when we call for help (v. 22b). And the end result is always good:

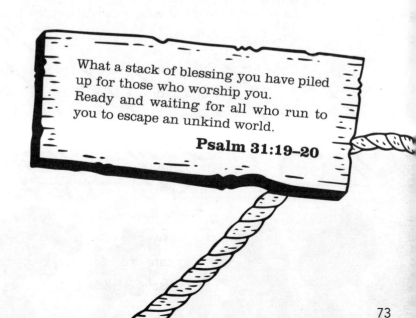

What a stack of blessing you have piled up for those who worship you. Ready and waiting for all who run to you to escape an unkind world.

Psalm 31:19–20

EYES FRONT

Henry Ford was right: 'When everything seems to be going against you, remember that the airplane takes off against the wind, not with it!'[6]

STRUGGLES ARE A PART OF LIFE,

so it's comforting to read words like these from someone as great as King David: 'I am in trouble,' he wrote. 'My eye is clouded and weakened by grief, my soul and my body also' (Psalm 31:9 AMP). Nobody can go through life without moments like these. But if we read on we see another essential truth: in the tough times we find out the most about where our trust lies.

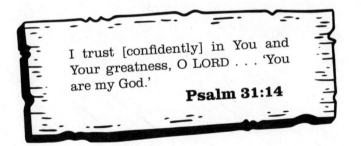

I trust [confidently] in You and Your greatness, O LORD . . . 'You are my God.'

Psalm 31:14

When hard times come, it's tempting to look back and long for things to be the way they were. But we are called always to look forward, not back. That's where God is leading us. Look up, not down – ahead, not back. That's where our help comes from, and that's where our courage gets restored and renewed.

Living Well with Others

Good relationships are key to every aspect of our lives – school, home and play. They matter and they affect our lives in every way.

For example, one of the strongest motivations for me to do my best work is the team I work with, especially the filming crew. We're like brothers and sisters. We've grown up together, seen each other get married, have children and juggle the game of life, family, work and risk, all together. We know each other's frailties and vulnerabilities, whether that's time away from home, the fear of jumping out of a plane or just finding it really hard to keep going after we've been working in the rain for a long time. I like to see us as a crew of imperfect warriors who always have each other's backs.

The best relationships are the ones where you don't have to hide the cracks and the flaws. You love those people not because they're brilliant, but because of who they are and what you've been through together.

Without good, honest relationships, humans grow anxious. If we don't allow others to know us with all our failings, we'll look in the mirror and only see the 'behind the scenes' version of ourselves in all its mess. And when we look at other people all we will see is their 'show reel' of highlights.

God's way is different. When we find love and acceptance in Christ, we don't need to try to impress others with our lives. We can be vulnerable and real with God and others. That in turn creates and strengthens bonds with those around us. We can forgive because we have been forgiven. We protect, give, help and support because we have found all that and more in the Almighty.

LOVE EACH OTHER AS I HAVE LOVED YOU.

JOHN 15:12

LIVING WELL WITH OTHERS

START WITH THE CLOSEST

Our words, actions and attitudes have the power to transform lives for the better. They can bring healing to people, communities and even nations. Our lives should be guided by Jesus' Golden Rule (Matthew 7:12):

> DO TO OTHERS WHAT YOU WOULD HAVE THEM DO TO YOU.

As John Wesley said, you should work hard to 'do all the good you can, by all the means you can, in all the ways you can, in all the places you can, at all the times you can, to all the people you can, as long as you can'.[7]

So how do we do this? It seems an impossible task. Well, we don't do it alone. The burden does not rest on our shoulders. That's why God

SENT US HIS HELPER,

the Holy Spirit.

> He gave us a good bath, and we came out of it new people, washed inside and out by the Holy Spirit. Our Saviour Jesus poured out new life so generously. God's gift has restored our relationship with him and given us back our lives.
>
> **Titus 3:5–7 MSG**

We don't achieve much impact on our own. But when we have the humility to kneel before the Almighty, He gives us all the power we need to change our world for the better. And where do we begin? Always with those closest to us.

9,100 FEET UP

Mount Hermon is vast. If you're in northern Israel and look north, you'll see it. It sits way up on the border between Syria and Lebanon and reaches 9,100 feet, which means that most of the year there's snow on the peaks. The streams and rivers that flow from it, including the River Jordan, irrigate the land for hundreds of miles around.

So when the Bible describes unity as being like 'the dew on Mount Hermon' (Psalm 133:2 MSG), it's a powerful image, and its influence is clear to see. God loves it when people work together in unity. I have seen the positive results of unity so many times in families, in teams and communities, and even in nations.

How wonderful, how beautiful, when brothers and sisters get along!
Psalm 133:1 MSG

Just like the water that collects on the slopes of Mount Hermon, unity has the power to sustain life. If people like you and me choose to unite (and maybe at times to swallow our pride), we inherit God's blessing. Unity paves the way for His power to flow from one to the next, with no broken connections.

Let's be people who unite rather than divide. Then the blessing of God will fall on us.

No one has ever seen God; but if we love one another, God lives in us and his love is made complete in us.

1 John 4:12

Worry matters

'Worry', as Corrie ten Boom wrote, 'does not empty tomorrow of its sorrow. It empties today of its strength.'[8]

Life is so much harder to face when we worry. The answer is not trying to find a problem-free life.

NO ONE GOES THROUGH LIFE WITHOUT FACING THINGS THAT WORRY US.

What matters is how we deal with them.

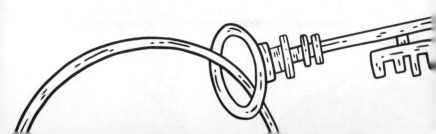

King David faced many difficulties in his life, and he wrote about them in Psalm 55. He described being betrayed by a close friend – a man with whom he had shared his secrets and trusted deeply. So David had a choice. Should he worry or should he turn to God?

As for me, I call to God, and the LORD saves me. Evening, morning and noon I cry out in distress, and he hears my voice.
Psalm 55:16–17

If you are involved in an argument with a close friend or family member, turn to God for wisdom, comfort and strength. Always do your best to forgive and to show grace. These things change so much and can strip an argument of its negative power. Whenever you feel the worry begin to build up, kneel down and lift it to God. We have a Father in heaven who cares.

Trust this promise:

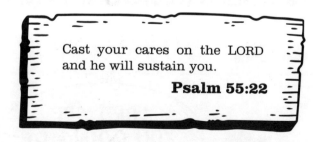

Cast your cares on the LORD and he will sustain you.

Psalm 55:22

That's a key secret to living well and to finding peace.

WASH ALL of me

I love this saying: 'Man is never as tall as when he kneels before God; and the man who kneels before God can stand up to anything.'

Not only does it go against so much of the so-called wisdom of today, it's also a powerful reflection of where true strength and humility lie. Strength comes from knowing our true place before God, knowing our need for forgiveness and trusting His promises for our life. Humility comes from knowing our need to be restored in our friendship with God.

I love the way Peter interacted with Jesus at the Last Supper:

LORD, ARE _YOU_ GOING TO WASH _MY_ FEET?

JOHN 13:6

Hot-headed Peter was appalled that Jesus would take on the role of a servant. Peter wanted to be the one who would do the washing. But that wasn't God's purpose. The purpose was for Jesus to show that all of humankind would need to be washed by Him, inside and out: you, me, everybody.

When Peter finally got it — that he had to let Jesus wash his dirty feet — he went all in, asking for not just a foot bath but a whole body wash (v. 9)!

I love it. I would be the same. When we understand that

GOD WANTS TO RESTORE AND REFRESH US,

to bring us home and to keep us close to Him for evermore, it changes our stubborn, numbskull hearts.

I think that's why Jesus loved Peter so much. And I think that's why He loves you and me.

STARTING OVER...AGAIN

We're all going to make mistakes at some point in our lives.

SOME of US will make ~~one~~ many.

What matters most is that we can admit when we've got ourselves into trouble, have the humility to say we are sorry, and then summon the determination required to start again.

King David found himself in trouble on multiple occasions. 'As for me, my feet had almost slipped; I had nearly lost my foothold.

For I envied the arrogant when I saw the prosperity of the wicked' (Psalm 73:2–3). But he also recognised when he slipped up. And time and time again, he found himself kneeling before God, humbly saying he was sorry. From this position, he realised how unbelievably blessed he was:

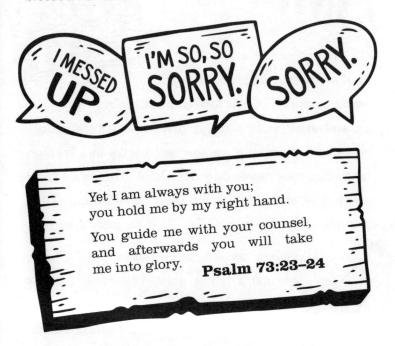

Yet I am always with you;
you hold me by my right hand.

You guide me with your counsel,
and afterwards you will take
me into glory. **Psalm 73:23–24**

Nothing compares to a strong relationship with God, rooted in forgiveness. When we rely on His guidance and strength, we have the power to overcome any obstacle – in our relationships, in our failures and our pride.

His
AMBASSADOR

Paul wrote that we are 'Christ's ambassadors' (2Corinthians 5:20). Being an ambassador is a great privilege. Ambassadors represent their king, queen or country in a foreign land. But they never operate alone. They gain their authority and power from their government. They act as spokespeople for their country's wishes.

Likewise, as an ambassador for Christ, we can't do it solo. We have to stay connected to the source every day afresh. In order to be effective and to have the strength to do our duty, we have to stay close to Christ.

Look to the LORD and his strength, seek his face always.

Psalm 105:4

Jesus gave His followers authority to work in His name (Luke 9:1) and invites us to ask for His help, promising that He will provide (John 14:13). Just think about that –

MOUNTAINS MOVED, LIVES HEALED, RELATIONSHIPS MENDED.

Love and forgiveness can change everything, and nothing is impossible for those who are found in Christ.

Even some of his earliest followers found these promises to be true:

I can do all this through him who gives me strength.

Philippians 4:13

As Christ's ambassadors, let's walk humbly, draw our daily resource from above, and be His representatives on earth – sharing goodness, kindness and love.

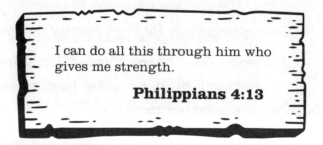

BEAUTIFUL FEET

People often ask the writer Shane Claiborne what Mother Teresa was really like in person. In his book *The Irresistible Revolution*, Shane explained that while some people wondered whether she had an angelic glow about her, the reality was much more mundane. He described her as a pretty standard, beautiful old granny: short, wrinkly, perhaps a little grouchy from time to time.

But one thing he said he'd never forget were her deformed feet. He'd stare at them and wonder whether perhaps she'd contracted leprosy.

One day he discovered the truth: whenever shoes were donated, Mother Teresa never wanted anyone to get stuck with the worst pair. She'd always dig through the pile and make sure she was the one who got the really broken, beaten-up shoes.

After years of living like this – loving her neighbour as herself – her feet were deformed.[9]

THAT'S GRACE.

That's sacrificial love in action. Selflessly putting others first.

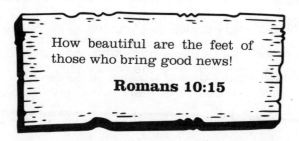

> How beautiful are the feet of those who bring good news!
>
> **Romans 10:15**

This is how, as men and women of faith, we stand out. We put others first, and with Christ inside us, we go the extra mile for people. We try to be Christlike. That's what Mother Teresa was doing: shining and sharing the light and love of Christ to people, always through her actions. Her feet reflected her heart – broken for the poor yet beautiful through her kindness.

Today, we ask Christ that our hearts and feet be instruments of love and courage in how we live.

GUARD YOUR WORDS

We all get angry sometimes, and we all say things we later regret. But be under no illusion, the words we say can cause a great deal of trouble. So be careful.

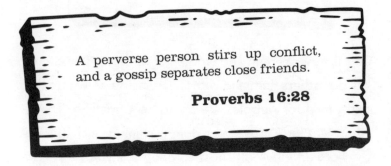

A perverse person stirs up conflict, and a gossip separates close friends.

Proverbs 16:28

(By the way, if you're ever unsure whether you're gossiping or not, ask yourself this: Will the person I am speaking to think less or worse of the person I am speaking about? If the answer's yes, then it's gossip, so leave it out.)

OUR WORDS CAN ALSO HEAL:

'A gentle response defuses anger' (Proverbs 15:1 MSG); 'Kind words heal and help' (v. 4 MSG); and, 'The soothing tongue is a tree of life' (v. 4). If we offer genuine encouragement to people, we're offering verbal sunshine, the sort of truth that can make people's day, even change their lives.

Ultimately, how you speak about others speaks loudest about yourself. (My mum taught me that.)

SO ALWAYS GUARD YOUR WORDS AND KNOW THEIR POWER TO BUILD UP OR DESTROY.

STARTING STRONG, STAYING TOGETHER

Each day I try my best to start out on my knees.

I remind myself to tackle the day with Christ first – that I am the glove and He is the hand; I try to listen and be still; then I read a little bit of the Bible, say thanks for all the good, and ask for help with all ahead. It takes me ten minutes or less, but it is where I get my soul fuel for the day and tasks ahead.

Wherever I am in the world, I also know that one of my closest friends, Jim, will be doing the same thing.

He, like me, is a busy guy, but he never misses a day. We do this together every single day, Christmas included. And each year, we commit to going again. We read the same verses and then send each other an email with any thoughts, struggles and feelings. This brotherhood is a source of lasting strength for us both.

HONESTY, FRIENDSHIP AND GROWTH ALL BELONG TOGETHER.

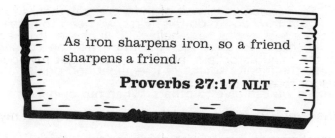

As iron sharpens iron, so a friend sharpens a friend.

Proverbs 27:17 NLT

We're not wired to live in isolation. We are designed to live in communities where love and friendship flow freely, where people of peace try to strengthen and support each other every day. This is how we grow and build strong foundations in our lives: through honest friendships, challenge, shared courage and enduring commitment. Thank you, Jim.

Be a Blessing Machine

We want to know that our life has meaning beyond just survival — beyond food, water and shelter. As children of Christ we are called to spread goodness and light, to bless people. A friend of mine often describes it as being a 'blessing machine'. I love that.

But how do we do this? First, we need to receive in order to give. And the more we can connect to the infinite source of love, light and power, the more we can give to others. When our own lives are overflowing with goodness, we can be more effective 'blessing machines'.

As the pastor Nicky Gumbel said, 'It is God's blessing on your life that enables you to make a difference to the lives of others. God is the source of all blessing. He loves to bless you.'[10]

WHAT GOD WANTS FOR YOU IS GOOD.

Life will not necessarily be easy, but you will not be able to improve on God's plan for you. He has known the intricacies of your life since long ago, and He will ultimately make all our lives beautiful. His promise is that He will always give you the energy you need to bless others:

> That energy is God's energy, an energy deep within you.
>
> **Philippians 2:13 MSG**

Let's draw on this and never tire of doing good in words, deeds, actions and attitudes. Together, let's daily fire up that blessing machine.

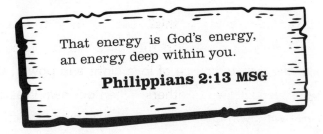

GOD'S Faithfulness

I'm so grateful for the fact that the two friends who were my best men at our wedding are still the guys I'd choose for the job today. Our friendship has grown even stronger over the years. It's a constant reminder of the power of faithfulness.

Faithfulness sounds like such an old-fashioned word. But it happens to be one of the most powerful forces on the planet. Like a river gradually smoothing out the rocks beneath it, faithfulness works slowly. But as we make the daily decisions to be loyal and loving to our family and good friends, our actions cannot fail to make a difference.

But it's not always easy. All relationships have their challenges, and faithfulness wouldn't be so powerful if it didn't cost us something. It is most important in our relationship with God. Being faithful to Him can be really hard sometimes. When doubts and fears and failures crowd in and threaten to overwhelm us, it is easy for our hearts to get turned. It is then that faithfulness counts the most.

It is one thing to believe that God loves everybody else, but it can be much harder to believe that God really loves each of us individually. But being faithful involves trust in God's promises for our lives.

IF YOU WERE THE ONLY PERSON WHO EVER LIVED. JESUS WOULD STILL HAVE DIED FOR YOU.

God is faithful to us in all circumstances, whether triumph or defeat. Receive that love and show that faithfulness to those around you. It will set you apart and help you shine.

O GOOD AND ALL-POWERFUL GOD, WHO CARES FOR EACH OF US AS THOUGH EACH WERE THE ONLY ONE.[11]

WALKING HUMBLY

BACK <u>TO</u>BASICS

Even though I've been on this journey of faith and love since I was a young man, every day I need to remind myself of the basics. Especially when it comes to living lightly, living freely and trusting in the love of God. We are not judged and excluded. Just loved, loved, loved. His grace silences our fears, our pride, our pain, our whimpers.

In his letter to the church in Rome, Paul reminds them that nothing 'will be able to separate us from the love of God that is in Christ Jesus our Lord' (Romans 8:39). We are loved, regardless of our failings, and nothing can tear us apart from this overwhelming, unstoppable force.

WE ARE LOVED.
NOT CONDEMNED.

When I remind myself of the truth that God loves and accepts us unconditionally, it changes my heart and my attitude. It guides me in how I want to live. Faithfulness is so beautiful when you know there's a loving Father cheering you on, calling you ever closer.

Even when the storms hit, we stay faithful because there is always a purpose, and we trust that **HE IS IN CONTROL.**

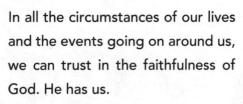

In all things God works for the good of those who love him, who have been called according to his purpose.

Romans 8:28

In all the circumstances of our lives and the events going on around us, we can trust in the faithfulness of God. He has us.

105

PERSEVERANCE

When a new motorway was built, taking passing traffic away from Colonel Sanders' restaurant, his business crumbled. The future looked bleak. About the only thing he had going for him was a mighty fine chicken recipe. Perhaps he could sell the recipe to other restaurateurs and earn a slice of every chicken meal sold. How hard could it be?

The answer: very.

His first day of appointments brought nothing but rejection. So did his second. And his third. In fact, Colonel Sanders knocked on 1,009 doors before someone gave him a yes and the legend and business empire that became Kentucky Fried Chicken was finally born.[12]

FAITHULNESS ISN'T ALWAYS EASY.

There are times when the setbacks get on top of us and we are tempted to give up. But when it is toughest, look up, don't give up:

I will give you every place where you set your foot . . . No one will be able to stand against you all the days of your life.

Joshua 1:3, 5

What a promise this is. In the battles of life it brings quiet assurance to know that we're empowered when we lean on God. Christ Himself and legions of angels cheer us on through the toughest times, always beside us, always bringing comfort and strength when we ask, ever onward towards the goal.

Let us run with perseverance the race marked out for us, fixing our eyes on Jesus, the pioneer and perfecter of faith.

Hebrews 12:1–2

The journey isn't always smooth. Faith and life itself require daily steps of courage and commitment. But faithfulness is always rewarded, and in Christ we are never alone.

the Hidden Team

Moses owed his life to five brave women. First were Shiphrah and Puah, the Jewish midwives who delivered him, defied Pharaoh and saved the lives of hundreds of male babies. Next was Moses' sister, Miriam, who was quick thinking and brave when she fetched Moses' own mother to nurse him. Then there was Moses' mother, who passed on great faith to her three children, Moses, Aaron and Miriam. Finally, and most surprisingly of all, there was Pharaoh's daughter, who had compassion on Moses. She was ultimately the one who rescued him and raised him as her own child.

Moses had no idea about the work that was going on behind the scenes to save him. But it was happening all the same. God was always at work.

Our lives are much the same.
We might have no idea about
what's going on behind the scenes,
such as how our words or actions or work fit
into God's plan, or what purpose that something
currently so painful might actually play in a happier
future. But we can know and trust in this promise:

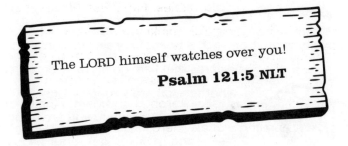

The LORD himself watches over you!

Psalm 121:5 NLT

He's the One who sees the bigger picture. Our role
is to trust Him and to have still hearts that can listen
for His voice, whether that comes through our hearts,
through His promises or through others. We can always
trust that Christ is working His purpose out through
our lives for the better.

Stay faithful and trust that His goodness will shine in
your life. Trust Him to do His work behind the scenes.

LOYALTY LASTS

Loyalty is something we all need in this world. Without it our families, businesses and communities, politics and even nations start to crumble.

Loyalty is built on such a beautifully simple concept: it declares that I am going to stick by you whether you are wrong or right, but I will tell you when you are wrong and help you get it right. I love friendships like that. I love it when people look out for me and let me look out for them. And I love the fact that Jesus always looks out for me. When I fall, stumble, trip and fail, His presence and forgiving arms help me to my feet and encourage me on.

Perseverance takes on new meaning when we have power beyond ourselves inside us. Christ is always with us. I have depended on this truth every day of my life of faith.

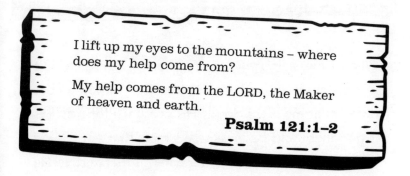

I lift up my eyes to the mountains – where does my help come from?

My help comes from the LORD, the Maker of heaven and earth.

Psalm 121:1–2

When we trust God and look to Him for the help we need in life, things get put right. Life starts to work the way it was supposed to. We have access to power we never knew before. Finally, we start to live freely, lightly and effectively. It all starts and ends with loyalty:

LOYALTY FROM US, LOYALTY FROM HIM.

Through good and bad, thick and thin, we are together. This is the foundation of all great relationships.

DYB. DYB. DYB.

When I mess up (which I do often), I can't help but feel distant from God. It's not that God withdraws but rather that my mess clouds His presence for me – as if goodness and badness don't mix. That's why God warns us to keep away from the things that hurt us. He gives us guidelines to follow:

LOVE EACH OTHER. FORGIVE EACH OTHER. GO THE EXTRA MILE FOR EACH OTHER.

LOVE, JUSTICE & MERCY. BE KIND.

We're given these guidelines for the simple reason that they protect us and He wants us to stay close to Him.

I want to make obedience to the way of love my default because I know that throughout time, God showers blessings on those who make faithfulness to Him their life. We will fail often, but God loves it when we do our best. That's why I love this verse:

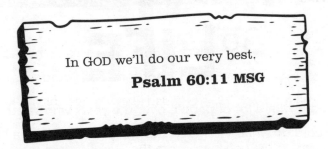

In GOD we'll do our very best.

Psalm 60:11 MSG

It's perfectly echoed by the promise that all Scouts make: to do your best (DYB. DYB. DYB). Maybe this verse is where Lord Baden-Powell, the Scouting founder, took this motto from. It's smart and it is good.

I am often struck by how many great organisations are, at heart, mere reflections of the path of God and the way of love. I like that. Today, let's choose that path of life and be faithful to Christ's words of love.

THE HARDER PATH THAT LEADS TO LIFE

I have met a lot of people over the years who say they would do whatever it takes to win a race or climb a big mountain. But just having the will to win isn't enough. In fact, those feelings mean nothing if we don't also have the will to train and the determination to do the hard work.

I love the story of Daley Thompson, the British decathlete who won gold at two Olympics. It was reported that his favourite day of the year to train was Christmas Day. He knew it would be the only day his competitors wouldn't be training. That is commitment, and it is part of why he won – he saw it as a chance to get 1/365th quicker than his rivals![13]

FINISH

Daley chose the harder path that led to success, and it made all the difference.

Being faithful to God is about making the difficult choices that ultimately bring us closer to the source of light, love and goodness. Choosing to be faithful rather than cheat, choosing to love rather than be jealous, choosing trust rather than fear, and kindness instead of selfishness. It isn't always easy to do this, but it is worth it. And the presence of Christ beside us will help us always.

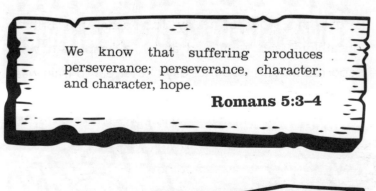

We know that suffering produces perseverance; perseverance, character; and character, hope.

Romans 5:3–4

SMALL BEGINNINGS

Everything big has to start small, and from God's perspective outside of space and time, who even knows what is small or insignificant anyway? Jesus said that faith as tiny as a mustard seed is enough to move a mountain (Matthew 17:20).

A mustard seed needs to be planted in the ground if it's going to start growing. Once planted, the growth is so strong it can even break through concrete. That's how it is with God.

HIS POWER CAN TRANSFORM ANYTHING.

Where we feel weak and fragile, when we see other people doing better than we are, God sees it all so differently. His perspective is not about achievement. It is always about love and edging us onward towards Him and towards home – ever stronger, ever closer.

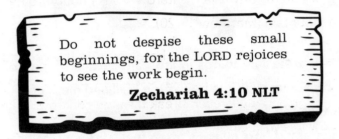

> Do not despise these small beginnings, for the LORD rejoices to see the work begin.
>
> **Zechariah 4:10 NLT**

Nothing you do for God in love goes unnoticed or unrewarded. You may not see the fruits today, tomorrow or even in this life, but if you're walking close to Christ, listening to Him and loving Him, you are accomplishing God's purpose for your life.

SO NEVER GIVE UP ON THE DREAMS

He has given you. They are gifts. Go for them, and don't be discouraged by small beginnings and many failures. Both those impostors are all too often signposts that you are doing something right and that His hand is leading you.

all for you

There are a few things in life I am certain of, and one thing above all is just how often I fail and mess up. Add to that the feeling of how small we are, and you can understand how humans often feel a little insignificant. Just look up at the night sky.

The Bible says that when compared to God, the people of this world — even its great leaders — are 'like grasshoppers' (Isaiah 40:22). He is the Creator of the entire universe, including the billions upon billions of stars (v. 26). Compared to Him 'the nations are like a drop in a bucket' (v. 15).

Yet here's the wonderful reality: He made it all for us. The universe and those stars are all for His children, and

HE LOVES US MORE THAN IT ALL.

The Lord Almighty is beside us: always close, always there to strengthen us when we are in need. He is quick to forgive and quick to save. Or as the Bible says:

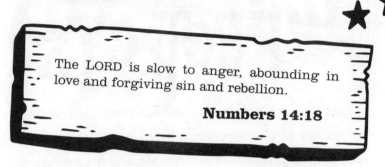

The LORD is slow to anger, abounding in love and forgiving sin and rebellion.

Numbers 14:18

It's All a Gift.

That's the entire radical, life-changing, life-affirming message of the Bible. God loves little us. So take comfort that despite our feelings and failures, Christ came for you and for me. He is beside us always, and He will not let us go.

Now when you see the stars in the sky, just smile in wonder. It is all for you.

LOYALTY PROTECTS

I love the fact that one of the fundamental founding principles of the Scouting movement is loyalty. It's a powerful expression of faithfulness, and it's a privilege to get to encourage and celebrate it in young people around the world.

FAITHFULNESS MELTS HEARTS AND STRENGTHENS RELATIONSHIPS.

And we all desperately need more of it in our lives. The Bible shows us what happens when we don't value faithfulness and loyalty. There is a pattern that gets repeated over and over again. It started when God blessed His people.

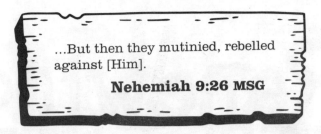

...But then they mutinied, rebelled against [Him].

Nehemiah 9:26 MSG

It's a pattern that's still familiar today. When we are not faithful to those around us, it hurts us and others. God doesn't ask us to be faithful to Him in order to restrict us. He encourages us to be faithful in order to protect us. God knows that faithfulness leads to prosperity. The more we show it, value it and protect it, the stronger and more beautiful that faithfulness becomes in our life.

We may fail in this many times, but God never does. He is always faithful. Often I have thanked God that His loyalty to me is so much greater than mine is to Him. And each time **HE RESTORES ME,** it makes me a little bit smarter and more determined to show loyalty and faithfulness in return.

Experience has taught me this simple truth: to be rich in life, be faithful.

Renewing our Strength

He gives strength to the weary
and increases the power of the weak . . .
But those who hope in the LORD
will renew their strength.
They will soar on wings like eagles;
they will run and not grow weary,
they will walk and not be faint.

Isaiah 40:29–31

How many times have I reminded myself of these
words when up against it in the wild, battling up
a mountain, and in those moments when I'm
simply struggling in life. Life can bring us all
to our knees.

But I always remember this great truth: a person is never as tall as when they kneel before God. And the person who kneels before God can stand up to anything. So wait on God faithfully and quietly. Let Him restore you, re-energise you and empower you to face everything you need to do.

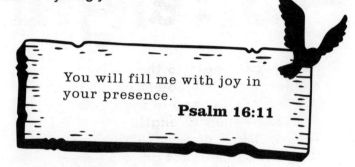

You will fill me with joy in your presence.

Psalm 16:11

Faith Changes Everything

It turns a hopeless end into an endless hope.

When You're 11 Years Old

and a friend dares you to do something cool but dangerous, it's hard to say no, even when your head says it's dumb and you can feel in your bones that it's a bad idea.

That's how I ended up trying to cross the muddy harbour near my home, on foot, at low tide. I'd never seen anybody else do it, and within the first ten steps I knew why. The thick mud and sludge clung to my limbs like cement. The further my friend and I went, the worse it got.

We just kept going, of course. But by the time we were about a third of the way out, we were stuck. Really stuck. We were chest deep in black, stinking clay, slime and mud, and we were exhausted.

Someone on the shore spotted us and called the lifeboat. Now I knew we were in trouble – whether we made it out or not. We wiggled and swam our way back, and as soon as we made it to the shore, only moments before the lifeboat crew launched, we split and ran home, both looking like monsters from the deep.

Of course my mother found out about it all and sent me around to the coxswain of the lifeboat's house to apologise in person, as well as offer myself to do chores for the crew in penance.

It was a good lesson that has served me well in so many survival situations: our decisions have consequences, so don't embark on any adventures without a solid back-up plan, and don't be egged on by others when your instincts tell you some- thing is a bad idea. It's called life wisdom. The smart person learns from it or, even better, learns it from others.

The Bible is full of wisdom, even for strong-willed hotheads. It shows us how to focus and direct our passions and how to take the very best type of risks. And above all, it always points us the way home to Christ and to love.

The greatest wisdom we can have starts with fear of the Lord: respect for the Almighty and His truths. Because if we truly fear God (in that biblical sense of holy respect), we need fear nothing and no one else.

Oh, and don't try and cross harbours at low tide when you know it is stupid!

TRUE FREEDOM

COUNTER-CULTURE WISE

The more of life I do, the more I realise the importance of wisdom. That's why I love these verses from Proverbs:

> Take hold of my words with all your heart;
> keep my commands, and you will live.
> Get wisdom, get understanding;
> do not forget my words or turn away
> from them.
> **Proverbs 4:4–5**

They remind me that wisdom isn't about making us look clever; its purpose is to bring us into a fuller, deeper, richer experience of life. And the wisdom that God gives is powerful. There's nothing like it:

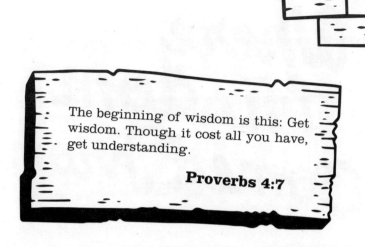

The beginning of wisdom is this: Get wisdom. Though it cost all you have, get understanding.

Proverbs 4:7

Wisdom isn't about intellect or exam results or awards. It is about knowing our need for forgiveness, the humility to ask for God's help, and the courage to walk on faithfully, with the love of Christ as our compass.

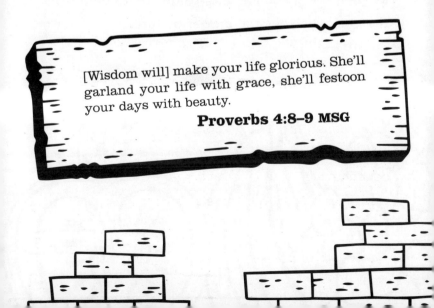

[Wisdom will] make your life glorious. She'll garland your life with grace, she'll festoon your days with beauty.

Proverbs 4:8–9 MSG

Where Wisdom Comes From

Knowledge, as many people have observed, is knowing that a tomato is a fruit. Wisdom is not putting it in a fruit salad! Knowledge is important, and it will help us in life, but knowledge alone does not have the power to save us. We need wisdom as well: the guidance and insight that come from the One who sees the bigger picture.

God promises always to provide wisdom whenever we search for it. He reveals it to us through the Bible, through experience, through His Spirit and through each other.

WE FIND WISDOM THROUGH OBSERVING AND LISTENING,

and we find it in our hearts, through that God-given instinct that helps us know what is smart, right and true. We also find it through prayer:

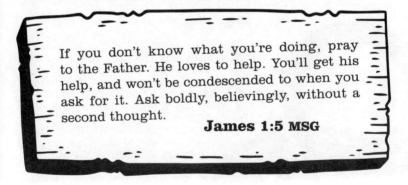

If you don't know what you're doing, pray to the Father. He loves to help. You'll get his help, and won't be condescended to when you ask for it. Ask boldly, believingly, without a second thought.

James 1:5 MSG

Seek wisdom in all of these places, and it will help keep you rooted in Christ, driven by love and secure in His grace.

THE POSITIVE PATH TO LIFE

When we operate outside of love, it can drain and destroy so much good in our lives. In my own life, I know that when I am angry, unforgiving or unkind, ultimately it saps all my energy. Negativity is a heavy weight to carry.

But if we always do our best to act in love and to seek God's truths for our lives, then we grow in character and freedom – we enjoy all the benefits of aligning ourselves with the greatest source of love and goodness in the universe.

NEGATIVITY

OPERATING IN THIS WAY
TAKES COURAGE AND COMMITMENT.

But the worthwhile things in life always do. That's why putting the positive fuel into our hearts and minds really matters every day.

So let's together be relentless in our determination to stay on the path that leads to life.

> Place these words on your hearts. Get them deep inside you . . . Teach them to your children. Talk about them wherever you are, sitting at home or walking in the street; talk about them from the time you get up in the morning until you fall into bed at night.
>
> **Deuteronomy 11:18–19 MSG**

the meaning of Life

According to the man whose signature appeared on almost every British banknote created during the 1990s, money isn't the answer. 'I am clear that the meaning of life can only be properly understood in the context of our relationship with God,' said Chief Cashier of the Bank of England, Graham Kentfield.[14]

His financial wisdom and authority gives these words such insight. The Chief Cashier knew that wealth alone does not have the power to satisfy us, let alone bring freedom to our lives. However much money you may acquire, it doesn't guarantee success in life.

As Jesus said, 'What good will it be for someone to gain the whole world, yet forfeit their soul?' (Matthew 16:26).

The way of true riches is to commit our way to God. Sometimes this brings money, sometimes not. But what is guaranteed is that following Christ always delivers spiritual riches. His plans for us are 'good, pleasing and perfect' (Romans 12:2).

PUTTING LOVE AND FAITH FIRST IN OUR LIFE BUILDS THE FOUNDATIONS FOR REAL HAPPINESS.

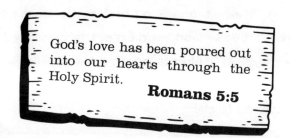

God's love has been poured out into our hearts through the Holy Spirit.

Romans 5:5

That's true wealth.

FREEDOM to FAIL

When I was a boy, my dad and I would sometimes hire a couple of horses and go riding on the beach near our home. They are some of my best childhood memories, even though there were many times I fell off onto the hard, wet sand.

I remember one time when I took yet another tumble and tears began filling my eyes. I felt annoyed and embarrassed to have fallen yet again. But just at that moment, my dad, with a big smile on his face, started to clap.

Applaud the fall? But why?

Dad wanted me to understand that I could become a good horseman only if I had fallen off a great number of times – that the only way to proficiency is through many failures.

In Christ we have something so special. We are set free from the fear of failure. There's no point in pretending we are perfect; our identity is found in being close to God – restored, empowered, set free.

THAT MEANS WE ARE FREE TO FAIL AND THEREFORE TO GROW.

It is the great irony: once we lose the fear of failure, we grow stronger and more competent in all we do. Always remember this:

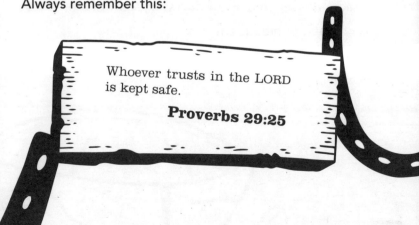

Whoever trusts in the LORD is kept safe.

Proverbs 29:25

CRacKed VeSSels

There's a beautiful art form in Japan called kintsugi. Instead of broken pottery being thrown away, the pieces are carefully glued together using a lacquer mixed with gold. The cracks are not covered over – they're revealed, celebrated.

It is our many cracks that make us human. We mess up, we carry damage, and we fall down and get broken. Cracks are simply part of that story, part of life. There is no need to hide them.

And yet hiding is exactly what a lot of us do.

When we pretend to be perfect, it is living a lie. And it denies Christ His purpose to redeem and rescue us, to set us free. Indeed, the light needs our cracks to shine through. Our failings remind us of our great need for Christ.

THE CRACKS ARE ACTUALLY MADE BEAUTIFUL BY THE LIGHT.

That's why God never completely removed whatever it was that Paul called his 'thorn in my flesh' (2 Corinthians 12:7). It kept Paul humble and leaning every day on the grace of God.

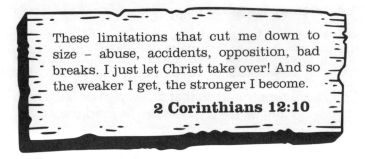

> These limitations that cut me down to size – abuse, accidents, opposition, bad breaks. I just let Christ take over! And so the weaker I get, the stronger I become.
>
> **2 Corinthians 12:10**

The point of true strength starts with humility and knowing our great need for Christ within us. This was the source of all of Paul's power and effectiveness.

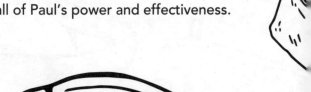

Your True ID

Who is 'the real me' or 'the real you'?

So much of what we see online or on TV is just the polished, shiny versions of people – not who they really are.

And often we put labels on people and they put labels on us – you're the smart kid, the chatty one, the one who's late, the one with spots, the musician...and sometimes these labels can be hard to shake.

But Jesus always sees beyond the labels, right into our hearts.

You are a chosen people . . . God's special possession . . . called . . . out of darkness into his wonderful light.
1 Peter 2:9

One of my favourite bits of the Bible is a little-known phrase that the disciple John used to describe himself time and time again. Instead of using his own

name, John would refer to himself simply as the one Jesus loved.

It's genius because when we see ourselves as simply a child of God, deeply loved and truly free, it changes everything. We are no longer our label; we are His, and that's all we ever need to know. That's the important part of our identity.

The answer to self-image comes flowing through these simple words:

It's in Christ that we find out who we are and what we are living for.

Ephesians 1:11 MSG

That's a beautiful and empowered way to live.

The Shoulders of Giants

Sir Isaac Newton was a great man. He was a mathematician, physicist, astronomer, theologian and author, and even today he's still considered to be one of the most influential scientists of all time.

But Newton was wise enough to know the truth about his achievements. In a letter to his great rival Robert Hooke, he wrote that his work on the theory of gravity had been possible only because of the scholarship of those who had gone before him. 'If I have seen further it is by standing on the shoulders of giants.'[15]

I admire him even more for writing that. And I love the way it reminds me of these words of Jesus:

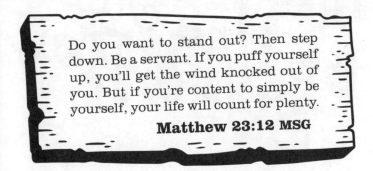

Do you want to stand out? Then step down. Be a servant. If you puff yourself up, you'll get the wind knocked out of you. But if you're content to simply be yourself, your life will count for plenty.

Matthew 23:12 MSG

But being humble doesn't mean that we hide away our gifts or fear standing out. Humility is simply part of living wisely.

Ultimately, we are standing on the shoulders of the greatest giant of all: Almighty God, who is always wanting to bless us, His children. What a gift!

I promise that I'll bless you with everything I have – bless and bless and bless!
Hebrews 6:14 MSG

Making the Universe Skip a Beat

Did you know that every time we express love and thanks to God — even if it's just a silent cry from deep within us — the whole universe quivers with delight? There are many references in the Bible to the stars and universe praising God:

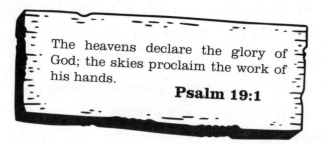

The heavens declare the glory of God; the skies proclaim the work of his hands.

Psalm 19:1

Even Jesus told us that if we ever stopped praising, the rocks themselves would cry out!

The whole crowd of disciples began joyfully to praise God in loud voices for all the miracles they had seen:

'Blessed is the king who comes in the name of the Lord!' . . . Some of the Pharisees in the crowd said to Jesus, 'Teacher, rebuke your disciples!' 'I tell you,' he replied, 'if they keep quiet, the stones will cry out.'
Luke 19:38–40

There have been times in my life when I've sensed this phenomenon for myself. I've sat watching the stars on a still night, or been high on a mountain or silently paddling down a remote jungle river at dawn. It is as if I can feel the rhythm of the universe and its delight in its Creator.

When our hearts sing like this with wonder, we join with billions of faith-filled men and women – those alive now as well as those in heaven. We add our heart songs to this epic crowd, a mighty family united in joy that Christ is alive and with us. It's the biggest picture, the greatest adventure, the wildest ride of our lives.

I like what C.S. Lewis wrote on the subject: 'How little people know who think that holiness is dull. When one meets the real thing . . . it is irresistible.'[16]

A life of faith is about life in full colour.

NEVER GIVE UP

At the end of this mini *Soul Fuel* journey through freedom, let's get back to the most life-enhancing, life-empowering, life-transforming message of all. When Jesus was facing His most agonising challenge – just hours away from death – He cried out these words:

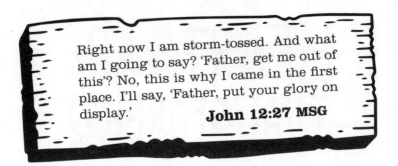

Right now I am storm-tossed. And what am I going to say? 'Father, get me out of this'? No, this is why I came in the first place. I'll say, 'Father, put your glory on display.' **John 12:27 MSG**

Jesus chose to keep going, not turn away. He chose to trust His Father above, not give in to fear and doubt. When facing a death He did not deserve, He decided to never give up.

Never give up. These are the words that turned the world around when Jesus died, and they continue to turn the world around today. When people of faith make up their minds to keep going, to keep sharing the love of Christ,

THE WORLD AROUND US IS TRANSFORMED.

RELATIONSHIPS ARE TRANSFORMED.

HEARTS ARE TRANSFORMED.

THE LOVE OF JESUS WINS.

So together let's start each day just as we did the last: knees down, eyes up. Get the good news in.

THE SECOND TIME

I saw the summit of Everest, I was alone. Instead of climbing the mountain, my friend Gilo and I were each flying a powered paraglider, which is basically just a parachute with a propeller engine strapped to your back. We were higher than anyone had ever flown a powered paraglider before. It was minus 65 degrees, oxygen levels were dangerously low, and we were still some five thousand feet below the summit.

Then, all of a sudden, Gilo's engine developed a fault and stopped. He had no choice but to glide down and turn back. I suddenly felt vulnerable and alone without my wingman. But I knew this was our chance. The weather and wind conditions were as good as we would ever get up there. For us both, I pressed on.

It was both humbling and terrifying to look down on those giant Himalayan peaks below me; they all

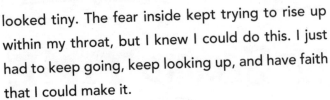

looked tiny. The fear inside kept trying to rise up within my throat, but I knew I could do this. I just had to keep going, keep looking up, and have faith that I could make it.

That expedition was worth the risk. We achieved a world first, we fulfilled the dream, and we came back alive and as friends. The adventure was successful.

If we want to live the fullest version of life possible, we need to become a ninja at dealing with risk.

We shouldn't try to avoid the scars that inevitably accompany risk and a life well lived. I'm covered with marks and scars, and they each tell a story. I like that. I've learned that life doesn't require us to be perfect and free of blemishes. What a waste that would be, bereft of history and endeavour. Life simply requires that we keep on giving of ourselves and that we keep getting back on our feet.

Life says not to fear the risk but to use it. Life reminds us that risk is the key to all growth and progress in life, love, faith and adventure!

CHAPTER SEVEN

TO ADVENTURE!

GET SET... GO!

Take a look at elite athletes like Roger Federer and Usain Bolt. Notice how they're able to raise their game those extra few percentage points when it matters most. When the stage is the biggest, when the pressure is at its greatest, when everything is on the line, these are the moments in which champions deliver. But when there's nothing at risk, it can be hard to achieve our best results.

The adventure of faith is undoubtedly the most exciting challenge that we humans can ever pursue. Alone, it is far beyond what we can achieve, but as the Spirit of God is with us, anything is possible.

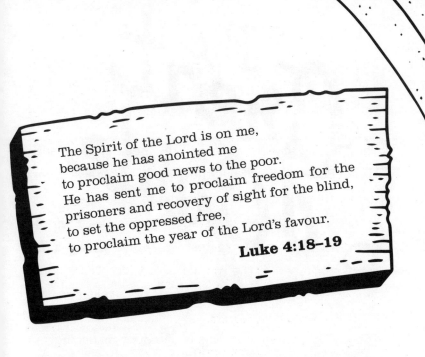

The Spirit of the Lord is on me,
because he has anointed me
to proclaim good news to the poor.
He has sent me to proclaim freedom for the
prisoners and recovery of sight for the blind,
to set the oppressed free,
to proclaim the year of the Lord's favour.

Luke 4:18–19

It's the ultimate adventure, and we're all included. God's Spirit will help us raise our game and fulfil all that potential He has stored in us. We just have to ask for His help. And on this adventure, our weakness isn't a hindrance. It is actually the key to relying on His strength alone, not ours.

SO, TAKE YOUR MARKS... GET SET...GO!

The Great Guide

Surviving in the mountains is all about managing risk and trusting the right people. As a young mountaineer, learning my trade, I encountered some great guides and a few less good ones. I learned so much about the mountains and survival through these experiences.

If we head off with an inexperienced guide, we will fast find ourselves in unnecessary danger and will make little progress. It is risk for the sake of risk rather than for any purpose. And ultimately we are more likely than not to end up in a ditch somewhere and probably injured.

But when we find a great guide, when we are ready to work hard and commit to trusting that person's decisions (even when they feel frightening), then we will travel far. Yes, there will be risk and danger, but we will be in safe hands and heading in a positive direction. And eventually we will reach that mountaintop, together, uninjured, and the place will take our breath away.

That's the key with life and with faith. Choose your guide wisely.

CHRIST IS THE ULTIMATE GUIDE,

and with Him all the risks are worthwhile. Wisdom and trust conquer dangers and risk.

The verse below has followed me on many adventures. It was written on a small scrap of paper, tucked away in the top of my pack, when I eventually stood on the summit of Everest at age twenty-three.

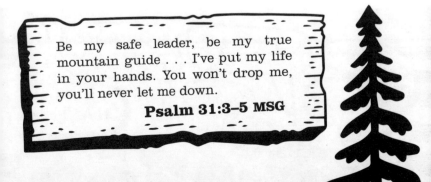

Be my safe leader, be my true mountain guide . . . I've put my life in your hands. You won't drop me, you'll never let me down.

Psalm 31:3–5 MSG

INCLUDE, Don't EXCLUDE

Of all the risks we can take, loving others can sometimes feel the most dangerous. The temptation is to surround ourselves only with people who are like us. But love can be so much bigger and bolder than that. Jesus hit the mark with this:

> If you love those who love you, what reward will you get? Are not even the tax collectors doing that? And if you greet only your own people, what are you doing more than others?
>
> **Matthew 5:46–7**

SHALOM

hey

YASSAS

GODDAG

ASALAAM ALAIKUM

ANYOUNG HASEYO

HEY

Instead, we're invited to take a risk and welcome and love all people, whether they're a different age, background, status or faith, or if they have a different outlook on life. We are called to include, not exclude.

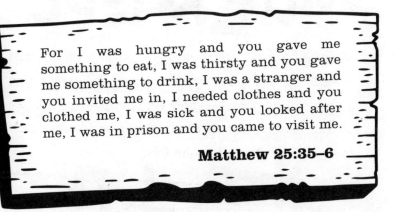

For I was hungry and you gave me something to eat, I was thirsty and you gave me something to drink, I was a stranger and you invited me in, I needed clothes and you clothed me, I was sick and you looked after me, I was in prison and you came to visit me.

Matthew 25:35–6

MANAGING CRISIS

I have always loved this observation: when written in Chinese, the word 'crisis' is composed of two characters. One represents danger, and the other represents opportunity.

When we find ourselves facing difficulty, it's right to be alert to the danger but also vital to think positively about the opportunities it presents.

The Bible adds a key third element to this equation that it often repeats:

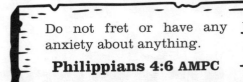

> Do not fret or have any anxiety about anything.
>
> **Philippians 4:6 AMPC**

That's a strong command that allows us to face both crisis and opportunity with courage and confidence. But how?

> In every circumstance and in everything, by prayer and petition . . . with thanksgiving, continue to make your wants known to God.
>
> **Philippians 4:6 AMPC**

And when we do that, here's the result:

> And God's peace . . . which transcends all understanding shall garrison and mount guard over your hearts and minds in Christ Jesus.
>
> **Philippians 4:7 AMPC**

Crisis is both danger and opportunity, but the key to managing them is laying them both before God, leaving worry behind, and then walking on in the peace and presence of Christ.

It's a smart formula for life.

THE GREATEST RISK

The greatest danger in life is to risk nothing.

If we are too cautious, we will never achieve anything. 'Whoever watches the wind will not plant; whoever looks at the clouds will not reap' (Ecclesiastes 11:4). We must try our best not to be daunted by obstacles. They are often opportunities in disguise. We must not be put off by wind and clouds.

Adventurers understand this. They know 'nothing ventured, nothing gained'. And it's true when it comes to how we use the tools that God has given us as well:

> Be generous: Invest in acts of charity. Charity yields high returns. Don't hoard your goods; spread them around. Be a blessing to others. This could be your last night.
>
> **Ecclesiastes 11:1–2 MSG**

If you're unsure about taking risks with and for God, just study the Bible. The more we give, the more we get. The more we give, the greater our wisdom grows. We have to keep giving because even if it doesn't seem to come back to us, it does. It will. It is impossible to sow in the kingdom of God and not reap a greater harvest.

This is one of the fundamental laws of the universe: you can't out-give God, and everything we have was always His.

WE DON'T KNOW EVERYTHING, but WE KNOW ENOUGH

The Old Testament king Jehoshaphat had every reason to panic. Three armies had combined to launch an offensive against him, and they were already just a few days' march away. But Jehoshaphat was smart. For years he'd been strengthening the kingdom of Judah, forming alliances in the north and increasing the prosperity of his people. He was a good king with a good brain.

But as the armies marched closer, Jehoshaphat was also not afraid to stand up in the temple and call out to God: 'We do not know what to do, but our eyes are on you' (2 Chronicles 20:12).

IT TAKES COURAGE TO PRAY.

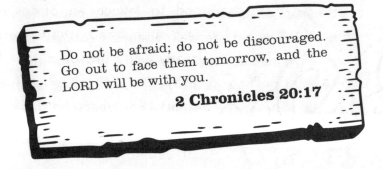

It takes courage to be vulnerable. It takes courage to bend the knee. But God responded to Jehoshaphat's prayer.

> Do not be afraid; do not be discouraged. Go out to face them tomorrow, and the LORD will be with you.
>
> **2 Chronicles 20:17**

This same promise applies to us today. God responds to prayer, and He is always with us. So when you're facing any risk, fix your eyes on the only power you can truly rely on.

LOOK CLOSER

Francis Collins, Director of the Human Genome Project, led a team of more than two thousand scientists who collaborated to determine the three billion letters in the human genome – our own DNA instruction book.

After years of painstaking research and dedication, one of the world's leading scientists reached this startling conclusion about the origins of life on earth: 'I cannot see how nature could have created itself. Only a supernatural force that is outside of space and time could have done that.'[17]

I love that all his knowledge and study led him to see something beautiful through all the data. That statement must have taken great courage, but it also showed incredible insight.

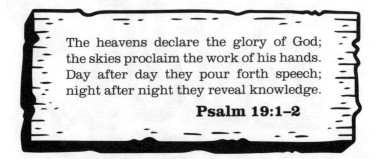

> The heavens declare the glory of God;
> the skies proclaim the work of his hands.
> Day after day they pour forth speech;
> night after night they reveal knowledge.
>
> **Psalm 19:1–2**

Faith should never be blind. Yes, sometimes faith involves a brave leap into the dark, but we don't have to be unthinking or unquestioning in order to believe in the Almighty.

GOD INVITES US TO LOOK, TO SEARCH, TO QUESTION

AND TO MEET CHRIST IN NEW AND SURPRISING WAYS ALONG THE WAY.

Science shouldn't be a stumbling block to faith. It should be a window. Our hunger for the truth shouldn't prevent us from asking questions. We are designed to explore, probe and seek knowledge. It is beautiful and heartening when we do so, and our

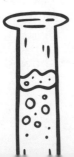

conclusions bring us back to what we naturally feel in our hearts. For me, it is that God is love and God is good.

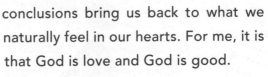

The Still Voice

Risky decisions come in many shapes and sizes — emotional, physical, social — but one thing they all have in common is this: they involve us having to step into the unknown. I love this verse from Isaiah:

> Whether you turn to the right or to the left, your ears will hear a voice behind you, saying, 'This is the way; walk in it.'
>
> **Isaiah 30:21**

It is telling that the voice is 'behind you'. It's not ahead of you or to the side. It's back out of sight, leaving you in front to take the leap of faith. That feels risky and takes courage, but right there is faith in a nutshell.

When we take the kind of risk that God invites us into, a life of adventure with Him, we have to accept that we won't always know exactly where we are going. The ultimate destination is clear, but the journey is the adventure.

EVEN THOUGH WE STEP OUT INTO THE UNKNOWN, WE ARE NOT ALONE.

There's always that voice behind us, whispering guidance and encouragement. We experience that guidance and encouragement in the promises of the Bible, through the sensation of the Holy Spirit, the wisdom of others and sometimes even through direct divine intervention. So let's always be alert to that still voice and bold in our response.

THINK BIG

We all want to make some sort of positive impact with our life, right? Whether this involves a handful of people or a whole nation, we all hope to leave the world a little better than when we entered it. But while it can be easy enough to daydream about the destination we'd like to end up at, taking those first steps can often be tricky. So just begin. Step out in faith. Make a plan and then take positive action to carry it out. If we don't take a few risks, we will never find out the true potential of the opportunities that we've been given.

When God gives us big goals, it often begins as a small idea. So protect and respect those dreams; they are often God-given. And remember: a mighty oak tree is just a little nut that held its ground. God likes it when we think BIG.

Like everything in this journey of faith and love, it comes back to the simple question: are we prepared to put our trust in God and step out with courage?

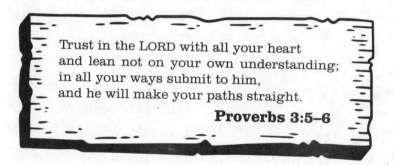

Trust in the LORD with all your heart
and lean not on your own understanding;
in all your ways submit to him,
and he will make your paths straight.

Proverbs 3:5–6

Know who to lean on and who to draw strength and resources from. And keep going through the storms. Never give up, because

YOU ARE BEAUTIFUL AND WONDERFULLY MADE.

Ready... Set...

God is preparing you for what He is calling you to do. This isn't a guess or some wise saying. This is the truth. God never sends people out on a mission without the right tools, and the deeper we go in this life of love and faith, the more power He gives us.

As we reach the end of this Soul Fuel journey, I hope that, at the very least, you've learned this: we can rely on God alone to give us the power we need each day. Just keep going back to the source. Keep asking God to empower you. Keep reminding yourself that God watches over you with love, pride and pleasure.

MISSION

The LORD your God . . . will rejoice over you with singing.

Zephaniah 3:17

Putting time and energy into our relationship with the Almighty is the smartest, most effective, most powerful thing we can do for our lives and our families. Let His truth and His presence steady you, let them settle you, provide you with a firm foundation, and calm and empower you for every day.

It's all a gift. Your gift. Soak it in.

WE CAN RELY ON GOD ALONE TO GIVE US THE POWER WE NEED EACH DAY.

THE STORM WAS A MONSTER.

It was night-time, and we were four hundred miles off the coast of Greenland, facing subzero, gale-force 8 winds, and waves as big as houses. Five of us were attempting to cross the frozen North Atlantic in a small, open rigid inflatable boat, and we were struggling.

It felt as if it was only a matter of time before one of the walls of roaring white water that were repeatedly smashing over us would capsize our little boat, and that would surely spell death so far from rescue in those arctic waters.

All five of us were truly terrified. I will never forget that sickening feeling of knowing we had really screwed it up – and we were going to die. Anticipating a horrible death was a genuine reaction to our situation.

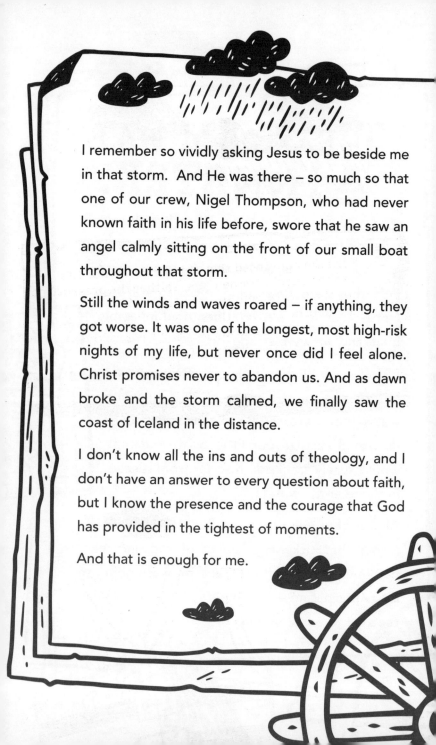

I remember so vividly asking Jesus to be beside me in that storm. And He was there – so much so that one of our crew, Nigel Thompson, who had never known faith in his life before, swore that he saw an angel calmly sitting on the front of our small boat throughout that storm.

Still the winds and waves roared – if anything, they got worse. It was one of the longest, most high-risk nights of my life, but never once did I feel alone. Christ promises never to abandon us. And as dawn broke and the storm calmed, we finally saw the coast of Iceland in the distance.

I don't know all the ins and outs of theology, and I don't have an answer to every question about faith, but I know the presence and the courage that God has provided in the tightest of moments.

And that is enough for me.

For I am convinced that neither death nor life, neither angels nor demons, neither the present nor the future, nor any powers, neither height nor depth, nor anything else in all creation, will be able to separate us from the love of God that is in Christ Jesus our Lord.

Romans 8:38-39

END NOTES

1. Elizabeth Hanly, 'Listening to Koko: A Gorilla Who Speaks Her Mind', Commonweal, 21 June 2018. Copyright © 2004 Commonweal Foundation, reprinted with permission. For more information, visit www.commonwealmagazine.org.

2. The Westminster Collection of Christian Quotations, ed. Martin H. Manser (Louisville: Westminster John Knox, 2001), p. 283.

3. The Cracked Pot', https://www.comp.nus.edu.sg/~tankl/ pot.txt.

4. Bill Hybels, Holy Discontent: Fueling the Fire That Ignites Personal Vision (Grand Rapids: Zondervan, 2007).

5. Nicky Gumbel, 'You Can Trust God', Bible In One Year, 1 February: Day 32 2018.

6. United States Army Recruiting Command, Recruiter Journal 49 (November 1996), p. 6.

7. Exact origins of this version of the quote are unknown, but John Wesley is believed to have said words to this effect in his 1799 sermons.

8. Corrie ten Boom, Clippings from My Notebook (Nashville: Thomas Nelson, 1982).

9. Shane Claiborne, The Irresistible Revolution: Living as an Ordinary Radical (Grand Rapids: Zondervan, 2016).

10. 'How to Be a Blessing Machine', Bible In One Year, https://www.bibleinoneyear. org/bioy/commentary/1021. Used with permission.

11. Saint Augustine, Confessions, 3.11.19.

12. Dennis Nafte, 'Colonel Sanders Failed 1009 Times Before Succeeding', Medium, 10 September 2017, https://medium. com/@dennisnafte/colonel-sanders-failed-1009-times-before-succeeding-ac5492a5c191.

13. Benjamin Lang, 'Christmas Day Training, Daley Thompson and the Path to Glory', Sports Gazette, 4 December 2018, https://sportsgazette.co.uk/christmas- day-training- daley- thompson- and- the- path- to- glory/.

14. Mick Woodhead, 'Foundations Daily', STC Sheffield, 27 February 2018, https:// stthomascrookes.org/talks/27- february- 2018/.

15. Letter from Isaac Newton to Robert Hooke, 5 February 1676, as transcribed in Jean- Pierre Maury, Newton: Understanding the Cosmos (New Horizons) (London: Thames and Hudson, 1992).

16. C. S. Lewis, Collected Letters: Narnia, Cambridge and Joy. Copyright © C.S. Lewis Pte. Ltd. 2006.

17. Francis Collins, The Language of God: A Scientist Presents Evidence for Belief (New York: Simon & Schuster, 2006), p. 67.

Bible Copyright Information

BEAR GRYLLS

OBE, has become known worldwide as one of the most recognized faces of survival and outdoor adventure.

Trained from a young age in martial arts, Grylls went on to spend three years as a soldier in the British Special Forces, as part of 21 SAS Regiment. It was here that he perfected many of the survival skills that his fans all over the world enjoy, as he pits himself against the worst of Mother Nature.

Despite a free-fall parachuting accident in Africa, where he broke his back in three places and endured many months in and out of military rehabilitation, Grylls recovered and went on to become one of the youngest climbers ever to reach the summit of Mount Everest.

He then went on to star in seven seasons of the Discovery Channel's Emmy Award-nominated *Man vs. Wild* TV series, which became one of the most-watched shows on the planet, reaching an estimated 1.2 billion viewers.

Since then he has gone on to host more extreme adventure TV shows across more global networks than anyone else in the world, including six seasons of the global hit TV show *Running Wild with Bear Grylls*.

His *Running Wild* guests have included President Obama, Will Ferrell, Ben Stiller, Roger Federer, Julia Roberts, Prime Minister Modi of India and many others stars.

He also hosts the Emmy-nominated INTERACTIVE Netflix series *YOU VS WILD* where it's the viewers who get to decide what adventure Bear goes on. This was one of the most viewed Netflix shows of the year, and is now in its second season.

In addition, Bear hosted the Emmy Award-nominated National Geographic landmark series *Hostile Planet* and Amazon's World's *Toughest Race* show.

He has also won two BAFTAS for his Channel 4 show *The Island with Bear Grylls* now in its sixth season.

His autobiography, *Mud Sweat and Tears*, spent 15 weeks at Number 1 in the Sunday Times bestseller list and he has written over 90 books, selling in excess of 18 million copies worldwide.

He is an Honorary Colonel to the Royal Marines Commandos, the youngest ever UK Chief Scout, and the first ever Chief Ambassador to the World Scout Organization, representing a global family of some fifty million Scouts.

He is married to Shara, and they live between a houseboat on the Thames in London and a private island off the Welsh coast.

Bear's life motto is simple:

Courage & Kindness AND NEVER GIVE UP!

To find out more about what Bear is up to,
discover other Bear Grylls titles
and outdoor gear made with best in class partners
head to www.BearGrylls.com

Inspiring and equipping you to get out there and find your adventure.

 @beargryllsOBE    @realbeargrylls   @beargrylls

Hodder & Stoughton is the UK's leading Christian publisher with a wide range of books from the bestselling authors in the UK and around the world. Having published Bibles and Christian books for more than 150 years, Hodder & Stoughton are delighted to launch Hodder Faith Young Explorers – a list of books for children.

Join us on this new adventure!

Visit **www.hodderfaithyoungexplorers.co.uk** to find out more.